This book belongs to

someone who is committed to

www.iamaluminary.com

The LUMINARY Journal

to Rise, Shine & Align

**THE COMPLETE
HEALTHY-HABIT-BUILDING
GRATITUDE JOURNAL**
for people who don't do
mornings, routines, or journals.

BY CHERYL B. ENGELHARDT

© 2019 Cheryl B. Engelhardt, CBE Music LLC
All rights reserved.

www.iamaluminary.com

THE LUMINARY JOURNAL TO RISE, ALIGN, & SHINE
The complete healthy-habit-building gratitude journal for people who don't do mornings, routines, or journals.

© 2018 CHERYL B. ENGELHARDT, CBE MUSIC LLC

All rights reserved. No part of this publication may be reproduced, distributed, or transmitted, in any form or by any means, including photocopying, recording, or other electronic or mechanical methods, without prior written permission of the publisher, except in the case of brief quotations embodied in critical reviews and certain other noncommercial uses permitted by copyright law.

DEDICATIONS

To my dad, the first entrepreneur I ever knew, though I never realized it. Thank you for continuing to inspire me to grow.

To my mom, who wakes up believing in me. This is the greatest gift.

To my husband, Silas, for requesting I find my alignment and for giving me the space to shine once I did. I'm writing this for you.

Warning:

Correct use of this book may result in a healthier body, more meaningful relationships, and an increase in productivity, compassion, leadership, peace of mind, and resilience.

How To Use This Journal

Thank you for being here and taking steps to create a grounded, peaceful, and luminous day.

The whole morning routine takes 18-28 minutes, with a few of the exercises occurring throughout the day. This is the order in which I do the routine:

- 2 minutes filling out the prompts for dreams, gratitude, etc.
- 5-10 minutes yoga with the Yoga Studio app
- 5-10 minute meditation with Simple Habit (inthekey.co/habit)
- 6 minutes of affirmations with one of my "Luminary" audio tracks. (www.iamaluminary.com)
- Acknowledgement, Exercise, and my Blank of the day happen throughout my day. I check them off the following morning.

More details about each section in the journal pages:

On the top of each page is a **Manifestation Mantra**. I like to keep the same mantra for at least 3 weeks to form the habit in my brain. This mantra could be related to a current goal or to creating a specific result in your life. It could be an affirmation of encouragement, strength, or peace. It can be a reminder of who you know you are, but struggle with being minute to minute.

Under the Manifestation Mantra is space to write the **date** and three things you're currently **grateful** for. This is where we train our subconscious to look for the good, thus attracting it.

Next, fill out the right column. Jot down the basic themes and visions from any **dreams** you can remember. You don't need details, just extrapolate the lesson and key figures or locations to remind you of the dream later and to make sure you've acknowledged the subconscious voice at work.

The **Best 24-Hour Moment** is a place for you to write your favorite moment in the last day. Doing so recalls the good feelings and brain chemicals that were released when the good thing was happening. This is part of training your brain to look for the good in every day. (This is especially powerful for us "fixers" - those who walk in to a room and see *everything* that is broken!)

Next, write the one thing you will **Accomplish** today. Of course, you're welcome to write more than one thing, but to keep it simple and focused, I like to have this section be the *one* thing I'll do, no matter what. Writing it down puts it in the universe, causing the task to get out of my head and onto paper… in reality.

The **Growth** section is an interesting one for me. I initially called it "Improve", but that implied that I wasn't already perfect. You are perfect, just as you are, right now. AND, growth and expansion is an important part of the human process. So, write one way you could grow today. Perhaps that's by being kind to a colleague who bothers you. Perhaps that's by putting $10 extra dollars into your savings account. Perhaps it's by learning something new, or simply filling out all of the check boxes on the left. Sometimes I write "focus", "patience", or "take time to rest."

The **checkboxes on the left** are meant to be checked off as you do them. This is because not everyone likes to exercise in the morning, and that acknowledgement often happens with other people, later in the day, when you are able to express gratitude for someone else

The **blank space** is for you to fill out anything else you'd like to make sure you do regularly. For me, I'll write "create something" or "send a kind text" or "sugar-free day" or "write another 750 words in my book", and I'll change it up every month or so, almost like giving myself a 30-day challenge.

If you take these few minutes as soon as you rise to focus, reflect, and assess, you'll be setting yourself up for a day of alignment, from which you will shine.

If you've forgotten the language of gratitude, you'll never be on speaking terms with happiness.
-Unknown

*Tomorrow is a mystery.
Today is a gift.
That is why it is called the present.*
-Eleanor Roosevelt

People will never forget how you made them feel.
-Maya Angelou

The measure of intelligence is the ability to change.
-Albert Einstein

and

Ingratitude is monstrous.
-William Shakespeare

Manifestation Mantra:

DATE:

I'M GRATEFUL FOR…

1

2

3

- ☐ MEDITATION
- ☐ YOGA
- ☐ EXERCISE
- ☐ ACKNOWLEDGEMENT
- ☐ AFFIRMATIONS
- ☐ _____

DREAMS FROM LAST NIGHT:

MY BEST 24-HOUR MOMENT:

TODAY, I WILL ACCOMPLISH…

TODAY, I WILL GROW BY…

DATE:

I'M GRATEFUL FOR…

1

2

3

- ☐ MEDITATION
- ☐ YOGA
- ☐ EXERCISE
- ☐ ACKNOWLEDGEMENT
- ☐ AFFIRMATIONS
- ☐ _____

DREAMS FROM LAST NIGHT:

MY BEST 24-HOUR MOMENT:

TODAY, I WILL ACCOMPLISH…

TODAY, I WILL GROW BY…

For more inspiration, go to iamaluminary.com.

Manifestation Mantra:

DATE:

I'M GRATEFUL FOR…

1

2

3

- ☐ MEDITATION
- ☐ YOGA
- ☐ EXERCISE
- ☐ ACKNOWLEDGEMENT
- ☐ AFFIRMATIONS
- ☐ _____

DREAMS FROM LAST NIGHT:

MY BEST 24-HOUR MOMENT:

TODAY, I WILL ACCOMPLISH…

TODAY, I WILL GROW BY…

DATE:

I'M GRATEFUL FOR…

1

2

3

- ☐ MEDITATION
- ☐ YOGA
- ☐ EXERCISE
- ☐ ACKNOWLEDGEMENT
- ☐ AFFIRMATIONS
- ☐ _____

DREAMS FROM LAST NIGHT:

MY BEST 24-HOUR MOMENT:

TODAY, I WILL ACCOMPLISH…

TODAY, I WILL GROW BY…

For more inspiration, go to iamaluminary.com.

Manifestation Mantra:

DATE:

I'M GRATEFUL FOR…

1

2

3

- ☐ MEDITATION
- ☐ YOGA
- ☐ EXERCISE
- ☐ ACKNOWLEDGEMENT
- ☐ AFFIRMATIONS
- ☐ _____

DREAMS FROM LAST NIGHT:

MY BEST 24-HOUR MOMENT:

TODAY, I WILL ACCOMPLISH…

TODAY, I WILL GROW BY…

DATE:

I'M GRATEFUL FOR…

1

2

3

- ☐ MEDITATION
- ☐ YOGA
- ☐ EXERCISE
- ☐ ACKNOWLEDGEMENT
- ☐ AFFIRMATIONS
- ☐ _____

DREAMS FROM LAST NIGHT:

MY BEST 24-HOUR MOMENT:

TODAY, I WILL ACCOMPLISH…

TODAY, I WILL GROW BY…

For more inspiration, go to iamaluminary.com.

Manifestation Mantra:

DATE:

I'M GRATEFUL FOR...

1

2

3

- ☐ MEDITATION
- ☐ YOGA
- ☐ EXERCISE
- ☐ ACKNOWLEDGEMENT
- ☐ AFFIRMATIONS
- ☐ _____

DREAMS FROM LAST NIGHT:

MY BEST 24-HOUR MOMENT:

TODAY, I WILL ACCOMPLISH...

TODAY, I WILL GROW BY...

DATE:

I'M GRATEFUL FOR...

1

2

3

- ☐ MEDITATION
- ☐ YOGA
- ☐ EXERCISE
- ☐ ACKNOWLEDGEMENT
- ☐ AFFIRMATIONS
- ☐ _____

DREAMS FROM LAST NIGHT:

MY BEST 24-HOUR MOMENT:

TODAY, I WILL ACCOMPLISH...

TODAY, I WILL GROW BY...

Manifestation Mantra:

DATE:

I'M GRATEFUL FOR…

1

2

3

- ☐ MEDITATION
- ☐ YOGA
- ☐ EXERCISE
- ☐ ACKNOWLEDGEMENT
- ☐ AFFIRMATIONS
- ☐ _____

DREAMS FROM LAST NIGHT:

MY BEST 24-HOUR MOMENT:

TODAY, I WILL ACCOMPLISH…

TODAY, I WILL GROW BY…

DATE:

I'M GRATEFUL FOR…

1

2

3

- ☐ MEDITATION
- ☐ YOGA
- ☐ EXERCISE
- ☐ ACKNOWLEDGEMENT
- ☐ AFFIRMATIONS
- ☐ _____

DREAMS FROM LAST NIGHT:

MY BEST 24-HOUR MOMENT:

TODAY, I WILL ACCOMPLISH…

TODAY, I WILL GROW BY…

For more inspiration, go to iamaluminary.com.

Manifestation Mantra:

DATE:

I'M GRATEFUL FOR...

1

2

3

- ☐ MEDITATION
- ☐ YOGA
- ☐ EXERCISE
- ☐ ACKNOWLEDGEMENT
- ☐ AFFIRMATIONS
- ☐ _____

DREAMS FROM LAST NIGHT:

MY BEST 24-HOUR MOMENT:

TODAY, I WILL ACCOMPLISH...

TODAY, I WILL GROW BY...

DATE:

I'M GRATEFUL FOR...

1

2

3

- ☐ MEDITATION
- ☐ YOGA
- ☐ EXERCISE
- ☐ ACKNOWLEDGEMENT
- ☐ AFFIRMATIONS
- ☐ _____

DREAMS FROM LAST NIGHT:

MY BEST 24-HOUR MOMENT:

TODAY, I WILL ACCOMPLISH...

TODAY, I WILL GROW BY...

Manifestation Mantra:

DATE:

I'M GRATEFUL FOR...

1

2

3

- ☐ MEDITATION
- ☐ YOGA
- ☐ EXERCISE
- ☐ ACKNOWLEDGEMENT
- ☐ AFFIRMATIONS
- ☐ _____

DREAMS FROM LAST NIGHT:

MY BEST 24-HOUR MOMENT:

TODAY, I WILL ACCOMPLISH...

TODAY, I WILL GROW BY...

DATE:

I'M GRATEFUL FOR...

1

2

3

- ☐ MEDITATION
- ☐ YOGA
- ☐ EXERCISE
- ☐ ACKNOWLEDGEMENT
- ☐ AFFIRMATIONS
- ☐ _____

DREAMS FROM LAST NIGHT:

MY BEST 24-HOUR MOMENT:

TODAY, I WILL ACCOMPLISH...

TODAY, I WILL GROW BY...

For more inspiration, go to iamaluminary.com.

Manifestation Mantra:

DATE:

I'M GRATEFUL FOR…

1

2

3

- ☐ MEDITATION
- ☐ YOGA
- ☐ EXERCISE
- ☐ ACKNOWLEDGEMENT
- ☐ AFFIRMATIONS
- ☐ _____

DREAMS FROM LAST NIGHT:

MY BEST 24-HOUR MOMENT:

TODAY, I WILL ACCOMPLISH…

TODAY, I WILL GROW BY…

DATE:

I'M GRATEFUL FOR…

1

2

3

- ☐ MEDITATION
- ☐ YOGA
- ☐ EXERCISE
- ☐ ACKNOWLEDGEMENT
- ☐ AFFIRMATIONS
- ☐ _____

DREAMS FROM LAST NIGHT:

MY BEST 24-HOUR MOMENT:

TODAY, I WILL ACCOMPLISH…

TODAY, I WILL GROW BY…

Manifestation Mantra:

DATE:

I'M GRATEFUL FOR...

1

2

3

- ☐ MEDITATION
- ☐ YOGA
- ☐ EXERCISE
- ☐ ACKNOWLEDGEMENT
- ☐ AFFIRMATIONS
- ☐ _____

DREAMS FROM LAST NIGHT:

MY BEST 24-HOUR MOMENT:

TODAY, I WILL ACCOMPLISH...

TODAY, I WILL GROW BY...

DATE:

I'M GRATEFUL FOR...

1

2

3

- ☐ MEDITATION
- ☐ YOGA
- ☐ EXERCISE
- ☐ ACKNOWLEDGEMENT
- ☐ AFFIRMATIONS
- ☐ _____

DREAMS FROM LAST NIGHT:

MY BEST 24-HOUR MOMENT:

TODAY, I WILL ACCOMPLISH...

TODAY, I WILL GROW BY...

Manifestation Mantra:

DATE:

I'M GRATEFUL FOR...

1

2

3

- ☐ MEDITATION
- ☐ YOGA
- ☐ EXERCISE
- ☐ ACKNOWLEDGEMENT
- ☐ AFFIRMATIONS
- ☐ _____

DREAMS FROM LAST NIGHT:

MY BEST 24-HOUR MOMENT:

TODAY, I WILL ACCOMPLISH...

TODAY, I WILL GROW BY...

DATE:

I'M GRATEFUL FOR...

1

2

3

- ☐ MEDITATION
- ☐ YOGA
- ☐ EXERCISE
- ☐ ACKNOWLEDGEMENT
- ☐ AFFIRMATIONS
- ☐ _____

DREAMS FROM LAST NIGHT:

MY BEST 24-HOUR MOMENT:

TODAY, I WILL ACCOMPLISH...

TODAY, I WILL GROW BY...

For more inspiration, go to iamaluminary.com.

Manifestation Mantra:

DATE:

I'M GRATEFUL FOR…

1

2

3

- ☐ MEDITATION
- ☐ YOGA
- ☐ EXERCISE
- ☐ ACKNOWLEDGEMENT
- ☐ AFFIRMATIONS
- ☐ _____

DREAMS FROM LAST NIGHT:

MY BEST 24-HOUR MOMENT:

TODAY, I WILL ACCOMPLISH…

TODAY, I WILL GROW BY…

DATE:

I'M GRATEFUL FOR…

1

2

3

- ☐ MEDITATION
- ☐ YOGA
- ☐ EXERCISE
- ☐ ACKNOWLEDGEMENT
- ☐ AFFIRMATIONS
- ☐ _____

DREAMS FROM LAST NIGHT:

MY BEST 24-HOUR MOMENT:

TODAY, I WILL ACCOMPLISH…

TODAY, I WILL GROW BY…

Manifestation Mantra:

DATE:

I'M GRATEFUL FOR...

1

2

3

- ☐ MEDITATION
- ☐ YOGA
- ☐ EXERCISE
- ☐ ACKNOWLEDGEMENT
- ☐ AFFIRMATIONS
- ☐ _____

DREAMS FROM LAST NIGHT:

MY BEST 24-HOUR MOMENT:

TODAY, I WILL ACCOMPLISH...

TODAY, I WILL GROW BY...

DATE:

I'M GRATEFUL FOR...

1

2

3

- ☐ MEDITATION
- ☐ YOGA
- ☐ EXERCISE
- ☐ ACKNOWLEDGEMENT
- ☐ AFFIRMATIONS
- ☐ _____

DREAMS FROM LAST NIGHT:

MY BEST 24-HOUR MOMENT:

TODAY, I WILL ACCOMPLISH...

TODAY, I WILL GROW BY...

Manifestation Mantra:

DATE:

I'M GRATEFUL FOR...

1

2

3

- ☐ MEDITATION
- ☐ YOGA
- ☐ EXERCISE
- ☐ ACKNOWLEDGEMENT
- ☐ AFFIRMATIONS
- ☐ _____

DREAMS FROM LAST NIGHT:

MY BEST 24-HOUR MOMENT:

TODAY, I WILL ACCOMPLISH...

TODAY, I WILL GROW BY...

DATE:

I'M GRATEFUL FOR...

1

2

3

- ☐ MEDITATION
- ☐ YOGA
- ☐ EXERCISE
- ☐ ACKNOWLEDGEMENT
- ☐ AFFIRMATIONS
- ☐ _____

DREAMS FROM LAST NIGHT:

MY BEST 24-HOUR MOMENT:

TODAY, I WILL ACCOMPLISH...

TODAY, I WILL GROW BY...

Manifestation Mantra:

DATE:

I'M GRATEFUL FOR...

1

2

3

- ☐ MEDITATION
- ☐ YOGA
- ☐ EXERCISE
- ☐ ACKNOWLEDGEMENT
- ☐ AFFIRMATIONS
- ☐ _____

DREAMS FROM LAST NIGHT:

MY BEST 24-HOUR MOMENT:

TODAY, I WILL ACCOMPLISH...

TODAY, I WILL GROW BY...

DATE:

I'M GRATEFUL FOR...

1

2

3

- ☐ MEDITATION
- ☐ YOGA
- ☐ EXERCISE
- ☐ ACKNOWLEDGEMENT
- ☐ AFFIRMATIONS
- ☐ _____

DREAMS FROM LAST NIGHT:

MY BEST 24-HOUR MOMENT:

TODAY, I WILL ACCOMPLISH...

TODAY, I WILL GROW BY...

For more inspiration, go to iamaluminary.com.

Manifestation Mantra:

DATE:

I'M GRATEFUL FOR…

1

2

3

- ☐ MEDITATION
- ☐ YOGA
- ☐ EXERCISE
- ☐ ACKNOWLEDGEMENT
- ☐ AFFIRMATIONS
- ☐ _____

DREAMS FROM LAST NIGHT:

MY BEST 24-HOUR MOMENT:

TODAY, I WILL ACCOMPLISH…

TODAY, I WILL GROW BY…

DATE:

I'M GRATEFUL FOR…

1

2

3

- ☐ MEDITATION
- ☐ YOGA
- ☐ EXERCISE
- ☐ ACKNOWLEDGEMENT
- ☐ AFFIRMATIONS
- ☐ _____

DREAMS FROM LAST NIGHT:

MY BEST 24-HOUR MOMENT:

TODAY, I WILL ACCOMPLISH…

TODAY, I WILL GROW BY…

Manifestation Mantra:

DATE:

I'M GRATEFUL FOR...

1

2

3

- ☐ MEDITATION
- ☐ YOGA
- ☐ EXERCISE
- ☐ ACKNOWLEDGEMENT
- ☐ AFFIRMATIONS
- ☐ _____

DREAMS FROM LAST NIGHT:

MY BEST 24-HOUR MOMENT:

TODAY, I WILL ACCOMPLISH...

TODAY, I WILL GROW BY...

DATE:

I'M GRATEFUL FOR...

1

2

3

- ☐ MEDITATION
- ☐ YOGA
- ☐ EXERCISE
- ☐ ACKNOWLEDGEMENT
- ☐ AFFIRMATIONS
- ☐ _____

DREAMS FROM LAST NIGHT:

MY BEST 24-HOUR MOMENT:

TODAY, I WILL ACCOMPLISH...

TODAY, I WILL GROW BY...

Manifestation Mantra:

DATE:

I'M GRATEFUL FOR...

1

2

3

- ☐ MEDITATION
- ☐ YOGA
- ☐ EXERCISE
- ☐ ACKNOWLEDGEMENT
- ☐ AFFIRMATIONS
- ☐ _____

DREAMS FROM LAST NIGHT:

MY BEST 24-HOUR MOMENT:

TODAY, I WILL ACCOMPLISH...

TODAY, I WILL GROW BY...

DATE:

I'M GRATEFUL FOR...

1

2

3

- ☐ MEDITATION
- ☐ YOGA
- ☐ EXERCISE
- ☐ ACKNOWLEDGEMENT
- ☐ AFFIRMATIONS
- ☐ _____

DREAMS FROM LAST NIGHT:

MY BEST 24-HOUR MOMENT:

TODAY, I WILL ACCOMPLISH...

TODAY, I WILL GROW BY...

For more inspiration, go to iamaluminary.com.

Manifestation Mantra:

DATE:

I'M GRATEFUL FOR...

1

2

3

- ☐ MEDITATION
- ☐ YOGA
- ☐ EXERCISE
- ☐ ACKNOWLEDGEMENT
- ☐ AFFIRMATIONS
- ☐ _____

DREAMS FROM LAST NIGHT:

MY BEST 24-HOUR MOMENT:

TODAY, I WILL ACCOMPLISH...

TODAY, I WILL GROW BY...

DATE:

I'M GRATEFUL FOR...

1

2

3

- ☐ MEDITATION
- ☐ YOGA
- ☐ EXERCISE
- ☐ ACKNOWLEDGEMENT
- ☐ AFFIRMATIONS
- ☐ _____

DREAMS FROM LAST NIGHT:

MY BEST 24-HOUR MOMENT:

TODAY, I WILL ACCOMPLISH...

TODAY, I WILL GROW BY...

For more inspiration, go to iamaluminary.com.

Manifestation Mantra:

DATE:

I'M GRATEFUL FOR…

1

2

3

- ☐ MEDITATION
- ☐ YOGA
- ☐ EXERCISE
- ☐ ACKNOWLEDGEMENT
- ☐ AFFIRMATIONS
- ☐ _____

DREAMS FROM LAST NIGHT:

MY BEST 24-HOUR MOMENT:

TODAY, I WILL ACCOMPLISH…

TODAY, I WILL GROW BY…

DATE:

I'M GRATEFUL FOR…

1

2

3

- ☐ MEDITATION
- ☐ YOGA
- ☐ EXERCISE
- ☐ ACKNOWLEDGEMENT
- ☐ AFFIRMATIONS
- ☐ _____

DREAMS FROM LAST NIGHT:

MY BEST 24-HOUR MOMENT:

TODAY, I WILL ACCOMPLISH…

TODAY, I WILL GROW BY…

For more inspiration, go to iamaluminary.com.

Manifestation Mantra:

DATE:

I'M GRATEFUL FOR...

1

2

3

- ☐ MEDITATION
- ☐ YOGA
- ☐ EXERCISE
- ☐ ACKNOWLEDGEMENT
- ☐ AFFIRMATIONS
- ☐ _____

DREAMS FROM LAST NIGHT:

MY BEST 24-HOUR MOMENT:

TODAY, I WILL ACCOMPLISH...

TODAY, I WILL GROW BY...

DATE:

I'M GRATEFUL FOR...

1

2

3

- ☐ MEDITATION
- ☐ YOGA
- ☐ EXERCISE
- ☐ ACKNOWLEDGEMENT
- ☐ AFFIRMATIONS
- ☐ _____

DREAMS FROM LAST NIGHT:

MY BEST 24-HOUR MOMENT:

TODAY, I WILL ACCOMPLISH...

TODAY, I WILL GROW BY...

For more inspiration, go to iamaluminary.com.

Manifestation Mantra:

DATE:

I'M GRATEFUL FOR...

1

2

3

- ☐ MEDITATION
- ☐ YOGA
- ☐ EXERCISE
- ☐ ACKNOWLEDGEMENT
- ☐ AFFIRMATIONS
- ☐ _____

DREAMS FROM LAST NIGHT:

MY BEST 24-HOUR MOMENT:

TODAY, I WILL ACCOMPLISH...

TODAY, I WILL GROW BY...

DATE:

I'M GRATEFUL FOR...

1

2

3

- ☐ MEDITATION
- ☐ YOGA
- ☐ EXERCISE
- ☐ ACKNOWLEDGEMENT
- ☐ AFFIRMATIONS
- ☐ _____

DREAMS FROM LAST NIGHT:

MY BEST 24-HOUR MOMENT:

TODAY, I WILL ACCOMPLISH...

TODAY, I WILL GROW BY...

For more inspiration, go to iamaluminary.com.

Manifestation Mantra:

DATE:

I'M GRATEFUL FOR...

1

2

3

- ☐ MEDITATION
- ☐ YOGA
- ☐ EXERCISE
- ☐ ACKNOWLEDGEMENT
- ☐ AFFIRMATIONS
- ☐ _____

DREAMS FROM LAST NIGHT:

MY BEST 24-HOUR MOMENT:

TODAY, I WILL ACCOMPLISH...

TODAY, I WILL GROW BY...

DATE:

I'M GRATEFUL FOR...

1

2

3

- ☐ MEDITATION
- ☐ YOGA
- ☐ EXERCISE
- ☐ ACKNOWLEDGEMENT
- ☐ AFFIRMATIONS
- ☐ _____

DREAMS FROM LAST NIGHT:

MY BEST 24-HOUR MOMENT:

TODAY, I WILL ACCOMPLISH...

TODAY, I WILL GROW BY...

Manifestation Mantra:

DATE:

I'M GRATEFUL FOR…

1

2

3

- ☐ MEDITATION
- ☐ YOGA
- ☐ EXERCISE
- ☐ ACKNOWLEDGEMENT
- ☐ AFFIRMATIONS
- ☐ _____

DREAMS FROM LAST NIGHT:

MY BEST 24-HOUR MOMENT:

TODAY, I WILL ACCOMPLISH…

TODAY, I WILL GROW BY…

DATE:

I'M GRATEFUL FOR…

1

2

3

- ☐ MEDITATION
- ☐ YOGA
- ☐ EXERCISE
- ☐ ACKNOWLEDGEMENT
- ☐ AFFIRMATIONS
- ☐ _____

DREAMS FROM LAST NIGHT:

MY BEST 24-HOUR MOMENT:

TODAY, I WILL ACCOMPLISH…

TODAY, I WILL GROW BY…

For more inspiration, go to iamaluminary.com.

Manifestation Mantra:

DATE:

I'M GRATEFUL FOR...

1

2

3

- ☐ MEDITATION
- ☐ YOGA
- ☐ EXERCISE
- ☐ ACKNOWLEDGEMENT
- ☐ AFFIRMATIONS
- ☐ _____

DREAMS FROM LAST NIGHT:

MY BEST 24-HOUR MOMENT:

TODAY, I WILL ACCOMPLISH...

TODAY, I WILL GROW BY...

DATE:

I'M GRATEFUL FOR...

1

2

3

- ☐ MEDITATION
- ☐ YOGA
- ☐ EXERCISE
- ☐ ACKNOWLEDGEMENT
- ☐ AFFIRMATIONS
- ☐ _____

DREAMS FROM LAST NIGHT:

MY BEST 24-HOUR MOMENT:

TODAY, I WILL ACCOMPLISH...

TODAY, I WILL GROW BY...

For more inspiration, go to iamaluminary.com

Manifestation Mantra:

DATE:

I'M GRATEFUL FOR...

1

2

3

- ☐ MEDITATION
- ☐ YOGA
- ☐ EXERCISE
- ☐ ACKNOWLEDGEMENT
- ☐ AFFIRMATIONS
- ☐ _____

DREAMS FROM LAST NIGHT:

MY BEST 24-HOUR MOMENT:

TODAY, I WILL ACCOMPLISH...

TODAY, I WILL GROW BY...

DATE:

I'M GRATEFUL FOR...

1

2

3

- ☐ MEDITATION
- ☐ YOGA
- ☐ EXERCISE
- ☐ ACKNOWLEDGEMENT
- ☐ AFFIRMATIONS
- ☐ _____

DREAMS FROM LAST NIGHT:

MY BEST 24-HOUR MOMENT:

TODAY, I WILL ACCOMPLISH...

TODAY, I WILL GROW BY...

For more inspiration, go to iamaluminary.com.

Manifestation Mantra:

DATE:

I'M GRATEFUL FOR...

1

2

3

- ☐ MEDITATION
- ☐ YOGA
- ☐ EXERCISE
- ☐ ACKNOWLEDGEMENT
- ☐ AFFIRMATIONS
- ☐ _____

DREAMS FROM LAST NIGHT:

MY BEST 24-HOUR MOMENT:

TODAY, I WILL ACCOMPLISH...

TODAY, I WILL GROW BY...

DATE:

I'M GRATEFUL FOR...

1

2

3

- ☐ MEDITATION
- ☐ YOGA
- ☐ EXERCISE
- ☐ ACKNOWLEDGEMENT
- ☐ AFFIRMATIONS
- ☐ _____

DREAMS FROM LAST NIGHT:

MY BEST 24-HOUR MOMENT:

TODAY, I WILL ACCOMPLISH...

TODAY, I WILL GROW BY...

Manifestation Mantra:

DATE:

I'M GRATEFUL FOR...

1

2

3

- ☐ MEDITATION
- ☐ YOGA
- ☐ EXERCISE
- ☐ ACKNOWLEDGEMENT
- ☐ AFFIRMATIONS
- ☐ _____

DREAMS FROM LAST NIGHT:

MY BEST 24-HOUR MOMENT:

TODAY, I WILL ACCOMPLISH...

TODAY, I WILL GROW BY...

DATE:

I'M GRATEFUL FOR...

1

2

3

- ☐ MEDITATION
- ☐ YOGA
- ☐ EXERCISE
- ☐ ACKNOWLEDGEMENT
- ☐ AFFIRMATIONS
- ☐ _____

DREAMS FROM LAST NIGHT:

MY BEST 24-HOUR MOMENT:

TODAY, I WILL ACCOMPLISH...

TODAY, I WILL GROW BY...

For more inspiration, go to iamaluminary.com.

Manifestation Mantra:

DATE:

I'M GRATEFUL FOR...

1

2

3

- ☐ MEDITATION
- ☐ YOGA
- ☐ EXERCISE
- ☐ ACKNOWLEDGEMENT
- ☐ AFFIRMATIONS
- ☐ _____

DREAMS FROM LAST NIGHT:

MY BEST 24-HOUR MOMENT:

TODAY, I WILL ACCOMPLISH...

TODAY, I WILL GROW BY...

DATE:

I'M GRATEFUL FOR...

1

2

3

- ☐ MEDITATION
- ☐ YOGA
- ☐ EXERCISE
- ☐ ACKNOWLEDGEMENT
- ☐ AFFIRMATIONS
- ☐ _____

DREAMS FROM LAST NIGHT:

MY BEST 24-HOUR MOMENT:

TODAY, I WILL ACCOMPLISH...

TODAY, I WILL GROW BY...

For more inspiration, go to iamaluminary.com.

Manifestation Mantra:

DATE:

I'M GRATEFUL FOR...

1

2

3

- ☐ MEDITATION
- ☐ YOGA
- ☐ EXERCISE
- ☐ ACKNOWLEDGEMENT
- ☐ AFFIRMATIONS
- ☐ _____

DREAMS FROM LAST NIGHT:

MY BEST 24-HOUR MOMENT:

TODAY, I WILL ACCOMPLISH...

TODAY, I WILL GROW BY...

DATE:

I'M GRATEFUL FOR...

1

2

3

- ☐ MEDITATION
- ☐ YOGA
- ☐ EXERCISE
- ☐ ACKNOWLEDGEMENT
- ☐ AFFIRMATIONS
- ☐ _____

DREAMS FROM LAST NIGHT:

MY BEST 24-HOUR MOMENT:

TODAY, I WILL ACCOMPLISH...

TODAY, I WILL GROW BY...

For more inspiration, go to iamaluminary.com.

Manifestation Mantra:

DATE:

I'M GRATEFUL FOR...

1

2

3

- ☐ MEDITATION
- ☐ YOGA
- ☐ EXERCISE
- ☐ ACKNOWLEDGEMENT
- ☐ AFFIRMATIONS
- ☐ _____

DREAMS FROM LAST NIGHT:

MY BEST 24-HOUR MOMENT:

TODAY, I WILL ACCOMPLISH...

TODAY, I WILL GROW BY...

DATE:

I'M GRATEFUL FOR...

1

2

3

- ☐ MEDITATION
- ☐ YOGA
- ☐ EXERCISE
- ☐ ACKNOWLEDGEMENT
- ☐ AFFIRMATIONS
- ☐ _____

DREAMS FROM LAST NIGHT:

MY BEST 24-HOUR MOMENT:

TODAY, I WILL ACCOMPLISH...

TODAY, I WILL GROW BY...

Manifestation Mantra:

DATE:

I'M GRATEFUL FOR…

1

2

3

- ☐ MEDITATION
- ☐ YOGA
- ☐ EXERCISE
- ☐ ACKNOWLEDGEMENT
- ☐ AFFIRMATIONS
- ☐ _____

DREAMS FROM LAST NIGHT:

MY BEST 24-HOUR MOMENT:

TODAY, I WILL ACCOMPLISH…

TODAY, I WILL GROW BY…

DATE:

I'M GRATEFUL FOR…

1

2

3

- ☐ MEDITATION
- ☐ YOGA
- ☐ EXERCISE
- ☐ ACKNOWLEDGEMENT
- ☐ AFFIRMATIONS
- ☐ _____

DREAMS FROM LAST NIGHT:

MY BEST 24-HOUR MOMENT:

TODAY, I WILL ACCOMPLISH…

TODAY, I WILL GROW BY…

Manifestation Mantra:

DATE:

I'M GRATEFUL FOR...

1

2

3

- ☐ MEDITATION
- ☐ YOGA
- ☐ EXERCISE
- ☐ ACKNOWLEDGEMENT
- ☐ AFFIRMATIONS
- ☐ _____

DREAMS FROM LAST NIGHT:

MY BEST 24-HOUR MOMENT:

TODAY, I WILL ACCOMPLISH...

TODAY, I WILL GROW BY...

DATE:

I'M GRATEFUL FOR...

1

2

3

- ☐ MEDITATION
- ☐ YOGA
- ☐ EXERCISE
- ☐ ACKNOWLEDGEMENT
- ☐ AFFIRMATIONS
- ☐ _____

DREAMS FROM LAST NIGHT:

MY BEST 24-HOUR MOMENT:

TODAY, I WILL ACCOMPLISH...

TODAY, I WILL GROW BY...

For more inspiration, go to iamaluminary.com.

Manifestation Mantra:

DATE:

I'M GRATEFUL FOR…

1

2

3

- ☐ MEDITATION
- ☐ YOGA
- ☐ EXERCISE
- ☐ ACKNOWLEDGEMENT
- ☐ AFFIRMATIONS
- ☐ _____

DREAMS FROM LAST NIGHT:

MY BEST 24-HOUR MOMENT:

TODAY, I WILL ACCOMPLISH…

TODAY, I WILL GROW BY…

DATE:

I'M GRATEFUL FOR…

1

2

3

- ☐ MEDITATION
- ☐ YOGA
- ☐ EXERCISE
- ☐ ACKNOWLEDGEMENT
- ☐ AFFIRMATIONS
- ☐ _____

DREAMS FROM LAST NIGHT:

MY BEST 24-HOUR MOMENT:

TODAY, I WILL ACCOMPLISH…

TODAY, I WILL GROW BY…

For more inspiration, go to iamaluminary.com.

Manifestation Mantra:

DATE:

I'M GRATEFUL FOR...

1

2

3

- ☐ MEDITATION
- ☐ YOGA
- ☐ EXERCISE
- ☐ ACKNOWLEDGEMENT
- ☐ AFFIRMATIONS
- ☐ _____

DREAMS FROM LAST NIGHT:

MY BEST 24-HOUR MOMENT:

TODAY, I WILL ACCOMPLISH...

TODAY, I WILL GROW BY...

DATE:

I'M GRATEFUL FOR...

1

2

3

- ☐ MEDITATION
- ☐ YOGA
- ☐ EXERCISE
- ☐ ACKNOWLEDGEMENT
- ☐ AFFIRMATIONS
- ☐ _____

DREAMS FROM LAST NIGHT:

MY BEST 24-HOUR MOMENT:

TODAY, I WILL ACCOMPLISH...

TODAY, I WILL GROW BY...

For more inspiration, go to iamaluminary.com.

Manifestation Mantra:

DATE:

I'M GRATEFUL FOR...

1

2

3

- ☐ MEDITATION
- ☐ YOGA
- ☐ EXERCISE
- ☐ ACKNOWLEDGEMENT
- ☐ AFFIRMATIONS
- ☐ _____

DREAMS FROM LAST NIGHT:

MY BEST 24-HOUR MOMENT:

TODAY, I WILL ACCOMPLISH...

TODAY, I WILL GROW BY...

DATE:

I'M GRATEFUL FOR...

1

2

3

- ☐ MEDITATION
- ☐ YOGA
- ☐ EXERCISE
- ☐ ACKNOWLEDGEMENT
- ☐ AFFIRMATIONS
- ☐ _____

DREAMS FROM LAST NIGHT:

MY BEST 24-HOUR MOMENT:

TODAY, I WILL ACCOMPLISH...

TODAY, I WILL GROW BY...

For more inspiration, go to iamaluminary.com.

Manifestation Mantra:

DATE:

I'M GRATEFUL FOR...

1

2

3

- ☐ MEDITATION
- ☐ YOGA
- ☐ EXERCISE
- ☐ ACKNOWLEDGEMENT
- ☐ AFFIRMATIONS
- ☐ _____

DREAMS FROM LAST NIGHT:

MY BEST 24-HOUR MOMENT:

TODAY, I WILL ACCOMPLISH...

TODAY, I WILL GROW BY...

DATE:

I'M GRATEFUL FOR...

1

2

3

- ☐ MEDITATION
- ☐ YOGA
- ☐ EXERCISE
- ☐ ACKNOWLEDGEMENT
- ☐ AFFIRMATIONS
- ☐ _____

DREAMS FROM LAST NIGHT:

MY BEST 24-HOUR MOMENT:

TODAY, I WILL ACCOMPLISH...

TODAY, I WILL GROW BY...

For more inspiration, go to iamaluminary.com.

Manifestation Mantra:

DATE:

I'M GRATEFUL FOR…

1

2

3

- ☐ MEDITATION
- ☐ YOGA
- ☐ EXERCISE
- ☐ ACKNOWLEDGEMENT
- ☐ AFFIRMATIONS
- ☐ _____

DREAMS FROM LAST NIGHT:

MY BEST 24-HOUR MOMENT:

TODAY, I WILL ACCOMPLISH…

TODAY, I WILL GROW BY…

DATE:

I'M GRATEFUL FOR…

1

2

3

- ☐ MEDITATION
- ☐ YOGA
- ☐ EXERCISE
- ☐ ACKNOWLEDGEMENT
- ☐ AFFIRMATIONS
- ☐ _____

DREAMS FROM LAST NIGHT:

MY BEST 24-HOUR MOMENT:

TODAY, I WILL ACCOMPLISH…

TODAY, I WILL GROW BY…

For more inspiration, go to iamaluminary.com.

Manifestation Mantra:

DATE:

I'M GRATEFUL FOR…

1

2

3

- ☐ MEDITATION
- ☐ YOGA
- ☐ EXERCISE
- ☐ ACKNOWLEDGEMENT
- ☐ AFFIRMATIONS
- ☐ _____

DREAMS FROM LAST NIGHT:

MY BEST 24-HOUR MOMENT:

TODAY, I WILL ACCOMPLISH…

TODAY, I WILL GROW BY…

DATE:

I'M GRATEFUL FOR…

1

2

3

- ☐ MEDITATION
- ☐ YOGA
- ☐ EXERCISE
- ☐ ACKNOWLEDGEMENT
- ☐ AFFIRMATIONS
- ☐ _____

DREAMS FROM LAST NIGHT:

MY BEST 24-HOUR MOMENT:

TODAY, I WILL ACCOMPLISH…

TODAY, I WILL GROW BY…

Manifestation Mantra:

DATE:

I'M GRATEFUL FOR...

1

2

3

- ☐ MEDITATION
- ☐ YOGA
- ☐ EXERCISE
- ☐ ACKNOWLEDGEMENT
- ☐ AFFIRMATIONS
- ☐ _____

DREAMS FROM LAST NIGHT:

MY BEST 24-HOUR MOMENT:

TODAY, I WILL ACCOMPLISH...

TODAY, I WILL GROW BY...

DATE:

I'M GRATEFUL FOR...

1

2

3

- ☐ MEDITATION
- ☐ YOGA
- ☐ EXERCISE
- ☐ ACKNOWLEDGEMENT
- ☐ AFFIRMATIONS
- ☐ _____

DREAMS FROM LAST NIGHT:

MY BEST 24-HOUR MOMENT:

TODAY, I WILL ACCOMPLISH...

TODAY, I WILL GROW BY...

Manifestation Mantra:

DATE:

I'M GRATEFUL FOR...

1

2

3

- ☐ MEDITATION
- ☐ YOGA
- ☐ EXERCISE
- ☐ ACKNOWLEDGEMENT
- ☐ AFFIRMATIONS
- ☐ _____

DREAMS FROM LAST NIGHT:

MY BEST 24-HOUR MOMENT:

TODAY, I WILL ACCOMPLISH...

TODAY, I WILL GROW BY...

DATE:

I'M GRATEFUL FOR...

1

2

3

- ☐ MEDITATION
- ☐ YOGA
- ☐ EXERCISE
- ☐ ACKNOWLEDGEMENT
- ☐ AFFIRMATIONS
- ☐ _____

DREAMS FROM LAST NIGHT:

MY BEST 24-HOUR MOMENT:

TODAY, I WILL ACCOMPLISH...

TODAY, I WILL GROW BY...

For more inspiration, go to iamaluminary.com.

Manifestation Mantra:

DATE:

I'M GRATEFUL FOR…

1

2

3

- ☐ MEDITATION
- ☐ YOGA
- ☐ EXERCISE
- ☐ ACKNOWLEDGEMENT
- ☐ AFFIRMATIONS
- ☐ _____

DREAMS FROM LAST NIGHT:

MY BEST 24-HOUR MOMENT:

TODAY, I WILL ACCOMPLISH…

TODAY, I WILL GROW BY…

DATE:

I'M GRATEFUL FOR…

1

2

3

- ☐ MEDITATION
- ☐ YOGA
- ☐ EXERCISE
- ☐ ACKNOWLEDGEMENT
- ☐ AFFIRMATIONS
- ☐ _____

DREAMS FROM LAST NIGHT:

MY BEST 24-HOUR MOMENT:

TODAY, I WILL ACCOMPLISH…

TODAY, I WILL GROW BY…

For more inspiration, go to iamaluminary.com.

Manifestation Mantra:

DATE:

I'M GRATEFUL FOR…

1

2

3

- ☐ MEDITATION
- ☐ YOGA
- ☐ EXERCISE
- ☐ ACKNOWLEDGEMENT
- ☐ AFFIRMATIONS
- ☐ _____

DREAMS FROM LAST NIGHT:

MY BEST 24-HOUR MOMENT:

TODAY, I WILL ACCOMPLISH…

TODAY, I WILL GROW BY…

DATE:

I'M GRATEFUL FOR…

1

2

3

- ☐ MEDITATION
- ☐ YOGA
- ☐ EXERCISE
- ☐ ACKNOWLEDGEMENT
- ☐ AFFIRMATIONS
- ☐ _____

DREAMS FROM LAST NIGHT:

MY BEST 24-HOUR MOMENT:

TODAY, I WILL ACCOMPLISH…

TODAY, I WILL GROW BY…

Manifestation Mantra:

DATE:

I'M GRATEFUL FOR...

1

2

3

- ☐ MEDITATION
- ☐ YOGA
- ☐ EXERCISE
- ☐ ACKNOWLEDGEMENT
- ☐ AFFIRMATIONS
- ☐ _____

DREAMS FROM LAST NIGHT:

MY BEST 24-HOUR MOMENT:

TODAY, I WILL ACCOMPLISH...

TODAY, I WILL GROW BY...

DATE:

I'M GRATEFUL FOR...

1

2

3

- ☐ MEDITATION
- ☐ YOGA
- ☐ EXERCISE
- ☐ ACKNOWLEDGEMENT
- ☐ AFFIRMATIONS
- ☐ _____

DREAMS FROM LAST NIGHT:

MY BEST 24-HOUR MOMENT:

TODAY, I WILL ACCOMPLISH...

TODAY, I WILL GROW BY...

For more inspiration, go to iamaluminary.com.

Manifestation Mantra:

DATE:

I'M GRATEFUL FOR…

1

2

3

- ☐ MEDITATION
- ☐ YOGA
- ☐ EXERCISE
- ☐ ACKNOWLEDGEMENT
- ☐ AFFIRMATIONS
- ☐ _____

DREAMS FROM LAST NIGHT:

MY BEST 24-HOUR MOMENT:

TODAY, I WILL ACCOMPLISH…

TODAY, I WILL GROW BY…

DATE:

I'M GRATEFUL FOR…

1

2

3

- ☐ MEDITATION
- ☐ YOGA
- ☐ EXERCISE
- ☐ ACKNOWLEDGEMENT
- ☐ AFFIRMATIONS
- ☐ _____

DREAMS FROM LAST NIGHT:

MY BEST 24-HOUR MOMENT:

TODAY, I WILL ACCOMPLISH…

TODAY, I WILL GROW BY…

Manifestation Mantra:

DATE:

I'M GRATEFUL FOR...

1

2

3

- ☐ MEDITATION
- ☐ YOGA
- ☐ EXERCISE
- ☐ ACKNOWLEDGEMENT
- ☐ AFFIRMATIONS
- ☐ _____

DREAMS FROM LAST NIGHT:

MY BEST 24-HOUR MOMENT:

TODAY, I WILL ACCOMPLISH...

TODAY, I WILL GROW BY...

DATE:

I'M GRATEFUL FOR...

1

2

3

- ☐ MEDITATION
- ☐ YOGA
- ☐ EXERCISE
- ☐ ACKNOWLEDGEMENT
- ☐ AFFIRMATIONS
- ☐ _____

DREAMS FROM LAST NIGHT:

MY BEST 24-HOUR MOMENT:

TODAY, I WILL ACCOMPLISH...

TODAY, I WILL GROW BY...

For more inspiration, go to iamaluminary.com.

Manifestation Mantra:

DATE:

I'M GRATEFUL FOR...

1

2

3

- ☐ MEDITATION
- ☐ YOGA
- ☐ EXERCISE
- ☐ ACKNOWLEDGEMENT
- ☐ AFFIRMATIONS
- ☐ _____

DREAMS FROM LAST NIGHT:

MY BEST 24-HOUR MOMENT:

TODAY, I WILL ACCOMPLISH...

TODAY, I WILL GROW BY...

DATE:

I'M GRATEFUL FOR...

1

2

3

- ☐ MEDITATION
- ☐ YOGA
- ☐ EXERCISE
- ☐ ACKNOWLEDGEMENT
- ☐ AFFIRMATIONS
- ☐ _____

DREAMS FROM LAST NIGHT:

MY BEST 24-HOUR MOMENT:

TODAY, I WILL ACCOMPLISH...

TODAY, I WILL GROW BY...

Manifestation Mantra:

DATE:

I'M GRATEFUL FOR...

1

2

3

- ☐ MEDITATION
- ☐ YOGA
- ☐ EXERCISE
- ☐ ACKNOWLEDGEMENT
- ☐ AFFIRMATIONS
- ☐ _____

DREAMS FROM LAST NIGHT:

MY BEST 24-HOUR MOMENT:

TODAY, I WILL ACCOMPLISH...

TODAY, I WILL GROW BY...

DATE:

I'M GRATEFUL FOR...

1

2

3

- ☐ MEDITATION
- ☐ YOGA
- ☐ EXERCISE
- ☐ ACKNOWLEDGEMENT
- ☐ AFFIRMATIONS
- ☐ _____

DREAMS FROM LAST NIGHT:

MY BEST 24-HOUR MOMENT:

TODAY, I WILL ACCOMPLISH...

TODAY, I WILL GROW BY...

Manifestation Mantra:

DATE:

I'M GRATEFUL FOR...

1

2

3

- ☐ MEDITATION
- ☐ YOGA
- ☐ EXERCISE
- ☐ ACKNOWLEDGEMENT
- ☐ AFFIRMATIONS
- ☐ _____

DREAMS FROM LAST NIGHT:

MY BEST 24-HOUR MOMENT:

TODAY, I WILL ACCOMPLISH...

TODAY, I WILL GROW BY...

DATE:

I'M GRATEFUL FOR...

1

2

3

- ☐ MEDITATION
- ☐ YOGA
- ☐ EXERCISE
- ☐ ACKNOWLEDGEMENT
- ☐ AFFIRMATIONS
- ☐ _____

DREAMS FROM LAST NIGHT:

MY BEST 24-HOUR MOMENT:

TODAY, I WILL ACCOMPLISH...

TODAY, I WILL GROW BY...

For more inspiration, go to iamaluminary.com.

Manifestation Mantra:

DATE:

I'M GRATEFUL FOR…

1

2

3

- ☐ MEDITATION
- ☐ YOGA
- ☐ EXERCISE
- ☐ ACKNOWLEDGEMENT
- ☐ AFFIRMATIONS
- ☐ _____

DREAMS FROM LAST NIGHT:

MY BEST 24-HOUR MOMENT:

TODAY, I WILL ACCOMPLISH…

TODAY, I WILL GROW BY…

DATE:

I'M GRATEFUL FOR…

1

2

3

- ☐ MEDITATION
- ☐ YOGA
- ☐ EXERCISE
- ☐ ACKNOWLEDGEMENT
- ☐ AFFIRMATIONS
- ☐ _____

DREAMS FROM LAST NIGHT:

MY BEST 24-HOUR MOMENT:

TODAY, I WILL ACCOMPLISH…

TODAY, I WILL GROW BY…

For more inspiration, go to iamaluminary.com.

Manifestation Mantra:

DATE:

I'M GRATEFUL FOR...

1

2

3

- ☐ MEDITATION
- ☐ YOGA
- ☐ EXERCISE
- ☐ ACKNOWLEDGEMENT
- ☐ AFFIRMATIONS
- ☐ _____

DREAMS FROM LAST NIGHT:

MY BEST 24-HOUR MOMENT:

TODAY, I WILL ACCOMPLISH...

TODAY, I WILL GROW BY...

DATE:

I'M GRATEFUL FOR...

1

2

3

- ☐ MEDITATION
- ☐ YOGA
- ☐ EXERCISE
- ☐ ACKNOWLEDGEMENT
- ☐ AFFIRMATIONS
- ☐ _____

DREAMS FROM LAST NIGHT:

MY BEST 24-HOUR MOMENT:

TODAY, I WILL ACCOMPLISH...

TODAY, I WILL GROW BY...

Manifestation Mantra:

DATE:

I'M GRATEFUL FOR…

1

2

3

- ☐ MEDITATION
- ☐ YOGA
- ☐ EXERCISE
- ☐ ACKNOWLEDGEMENT
- ☐ AFFIRMATIONS
- ☐ _____

DREAMS FROM LAST NIGHT:

MY BEST 24-HOUR MOMENT:

TODAY, I WILL ACCOMPLISH…

TODAY, I WILL GROW BY…

DATE:

I'M GRATEFUL FOR…

1

2

3

- ☐ MEDITATION
- ☐ YOGA
- ☐ EXERCISE
- ☐ ACKNOWLEDGEMENT
- ☐ AFFIRMATIONS
- ☐ _____

DREAMS FROM LAST NIGHT:

MY BEST 24-HOUR MOMENT:

TODAY, I WILL ACCOMPLISH…

TODAY, I WILL GROW BY…

For more inspiration, go to iamaluminary.com.

Manifestation Mantra:

DATE:

I'M GRATEFUL FOR...

1

2

3

- ☐ MEDITATION
- ☐ YOGA
- ☐ EXERCISE
- ☐ ACKNOWLEDGEMENT
- ☐ AFFIRMATIONS
- ☐ _____

DREAMS FROM LAST NIGHT:

MY BEST 24-HOUR MOMENT:

TODAY, I WILL ACCOMPLISH...

TODAY, I WILL GROW BY...

DATE:

I'M GRATEFUL FOR...

1

2

3

- ☐ MEDITATION
- ☐ YOGA
- ☐ EXERCISE
- ☐ ACKNOWLEDGEMENT
- ☐ AFFIRMATIONS
- ☐ _____

DREAMS FROM LAST NIGHT:

MY BEST 24-HOUR MOMENT:

TODAY, I WILL ACCOMPLISH...

TODAY, I WILL GROW BY...

Manifestation Mantra:

DATE:

I'M GRATEFUL FOR…

1

2

3

- ☐ MEDITATION
- ☐ YOGA
- ☐ EXERCISE
- ☐ ACKNOWLEDGEMENT
- ☐ AFFIRMATIONS
- ☐ _____

DREAMS FROM LAST NIGHT:

MY BEST 24-HOUR MOMENT:

TODAY, I WILL ACCOMPLISH…

TODAY, I WILL GROW BY…

DATE:

I'M GRATEFUL FOR…

1

2

3

- ☐ MEDITATION
- ☐ YOGA
- ☐ EXERCISE
- ☐ ACKNOWLEDGEMENT
- ☐ AFFIRMATIONS
- ☐ _____

DREAMS FROM LAST NIGHT:

MY BEST 24-HOUR MOMENT:

TODAY, I WILL ACCOMPLISH…

TODAY, I WILL GROW BY…

For more inspiration, go to iamaluminary.com.

Manifestation Mantra:

DATE:

I'M GRATEFUL FOR...

1

2

3

- ☐ MEDITATION
- ☐ YOGA
- ☐ EXERCISE
- ☐ ACKNOWLEDGEMENT
- ☐ AFFIRMATIONS
- ☐ _____

DREAMS FROM LAST NIGHT:

MY BEST 24-HOUR MOMENT:

TODAY, I WILL ACCOMPLISH...

TODAY, I WILL GROW BY...

DATE:

I'M GRATEFUL FOR...

1

2

3

- ☐ MEDITATION
- ☐ YOGA
- ☐ EXERCISE
- ☐ ACKNOWLEDGEMENT
- ☐ AFFIRMATIONS
- ☐ _____

DREAMS FROM LAST NIGHT:

MY BEST 24-HOUR MOMENT:

TODAY, I WILL ACCOMPLISH...

TODAY, I WILL GROW BY...

For more inspiration, go to iamaluminary.com.

Manifestation Mantra:

DATE:

I'M GRATEFUL FOR…

1

2

3

- ☐ MEDITATION
- ☐ YOGA
- ☐ EXERCISE
- ☐ ACKNOWLEDGEMENT
- ☐ AFFIRMATIONS
- ☐ _____

DREAMS FROM LAST NIGHT:

MY BEST 24-HOUR MOMENT:

TODAY, I WILL ACCOMPLISH…

TODAY, I WILL GROW BY…

DATE:

I'M GRATEFUL FOR…

1

2

3

- ☐ MEDITATION
- ☐ YOGA
- ☐ EXERCISE
- ☐ ACKNOWLEDGEMENT
- ☐ AFFIRMATIONS
- ☐ _____

DREAMS FROM LAST NIGHT:

MY BEST 24-HOUR MOMENT:

TODAY, I WILL ACCOMPLISH…

TODAY, I WILL GROW BY…

For more inspiration, go to iamaluminary.com.

Manifestation Mantra:

DATE:

I'M GRATEFUL FOR…

1

2

3

- ☐ MEDITATION
- ☐ YOGA
- ☐ EXERCISE
- ☐ ACKNOWLEDGEMENT
- ☐ AFFIRMATIONS
- ☐ _____

DREAMS FROM LAST NIGHT:

MY BEST 24-HOUR MOMENT:

TODAY, I WILL ACCOMPLISH…

TODAY, I WILL GROW BY…

DATE:

I'M GRATEFUL FOR…

1

2

3

- ☐ MEDITATION
- ☐ YOGA
- ☐ EXERCISE
- ☐ ACKNOWLEDGEMENT
- ☐ AFFIRMATIONS
- ☐ _____

DREAMS FROM LAST NIGHT:

MY BEST 24-HOUR MOMENT:

TODAY, I WILL ACCOMPLISH…

TODAY, I WILL GROW BY…

For more inspiration, go to iamaluminary.com.

Manifestation Mantra:

DATE:

I'M GRATEFUL FOR...

1

2

3

- ☐ MEDITATION
- ☐ YOGA
- ☐ EXERCISE
- ☐ ACKNOWLEDGEMENT
- ☐ AFFIRMATIONS
- ☐ _____

DREAMS FROM LAST NIGHT:

MY BEST 24-HOUR MOMENT:

TODAY, I WILL ACCOMPLISH...

TODAY, I WILL GROW BY...

DATE:

I'M GRATEFUL FOR...

1

2

3

- ☐ MEDITATION
- ☐ YOGA
- ☐ EXERCISE
- ☐ ACKNOWLEDGEMENT
- ☐ AFFIRMATIONS
- ☐ _____

DREAMS FROM LAST NIGHT:

MY BEST 24-HOUR MOMENT:

TODAY, I WILL ACCOMPLISH...

TODAY, I WILL GROW BY...

For more inspiration, go to iamaluminary.com.

Manifestation Mantra:

DATE:

I'M GRATEFUL FOR...

1

2

3

- ☐ MEDITATION
- ☐ YOGA
- ☐ EXERCISE
- ☐ ACKNOWLEDGEMENT
- ☐ AFFIRMATIONS
- ☐ _____

DREAMS FROM LAST NIGHT:

MY BEST 24-HOUR MOMENT:

TODAY, I WILL ACCOMPLISH...

TODAY, I WILL GROW BY...

DATE:

I'M GRATEFUL FOR...

1

2

3

- ☐ MEDITATION
- ☐ YOGA
- ☐ EXERCISE
- ☐ ACKNOWLEDGEMENT
- ☐ AFFIRMATIONS
- ☐ _____

DREAMS FROM LAST NIGHT:

MY BEST 24-HOUR MOMENT:

TODAY, I WILL ACCOMPLISH...

TODAY, I WILL GROW BY...

Manifestation Mantra:

DATE:

I'M GRATEFUL FOR...

1

2

3

- ☐ MEDITATION
- ☐ YOGA
- ☐ EXERCISE
- ☐ ACKNOWLEDGEMENT
- ☐ AFFIRMATIONS
- ☐ _____

DREAMS FROM LAST NIGHT:

MY BEST 24-HOUR MOMENT:

TODAY, I WILL ACCOMPLISH...

TODAY, I WILL GROW BY...

DATE:

I'M GRATEFUL FOR...

1

2

3

- ☐ MEDITATION
- ☐ YOGA
- ☐ EXERCISE
- ☐ ACKNOWLEDGEMENT
- ☐ AFFIRMATIONS
- ☐ _____

DREAMS FROM LAST NIGHT:

MY BEST 24-HOUR MOMENT:

TODAY, I WILL ACCOMPLISH...

TODAY, I WILL GROW BY...

For more inspiration, go to iamaluminary.com.

Manifestation Mantra:

DATE:

I'M GRATEFUL FOR...

1

2

3

- ☐ MEDITATION
- ☐ YOGA
- ☐ EXERCISE
- ☐ ACKNOWLEDGEMENT
- ☐ AFFIRMATIONS
- ☐ _____

DREAMS FROM LAST NIGHT:

MY BEST 24-HOUR MOMENT:

TODAY, I WILL ACCOMPLISH...

TODAY, I WILL GROW BY...

DATE:

I'M GRATEFUL FOR...

1

2

3

- ☐ MEDITATION
- ☐ YOGA
- ☐ EXERCISE
- ☐ ACKNOWLEDGEMENT
- ☐ AFFIRMATIONS
- ☐ _____

DREAMS FROM LAST NIGHT:

MY BEST 24-HOUR MOMENT:

TODAY, I WILL ACCOMPLISH...

TODAY, I WILL GROW BY...

Manifestation Mantra:

DATE:

I'M GRATEFUL FOR…

1

2

3

- ☐ MEDITATION
- ☐ YOGA
- ☐ EXERCISE
- ☐ ACKNOWLEDGEMENT
- ☐ AFFIRMATIONS
- ☐ _____

DREAMS FROM LAST NIGHT:

MY BEST 24-HOUR MOMENT:

TODAY, I WILL ACCOMPLISH…

TODAY, I WILL GROW BY…

DATE:

I'M GRATEFUL FOR…

1

2

3

- ☐ MEDITATION
- ☐ YOGA
- ☐ EXERCISE
- ☐ ACKNOWLEDGEMENT
- ☐ AFFIRMATIONS
- ☐ _____

DREAMS FROM LAST NIGHT:

MY BEST 24-HOUR MOMENT:

TODAY, I WILL ACCOMPLISH…

TODAY, I WILL GROW BY…

For more inspiration, go to iamaluminary.com.

Manifestation Mantra:

DATE:

I'M GRATEFUL FOR…

1

2

3

- ☐ MEDITATION
- ☐ YOGA
- ☐ EXERCISE
- ☐ ACKNOWLEDGEMENT
- ☐ AFFIRMATIONS
- ☐ _____

DREAMS FROM LAST NIGHT:

MY BEST 24-HOUR MOMENT:

TODAY, I WILL ACCOMPLISH…

TODAY, I WILL GROW BY…

DATE:

I'M GRATEFUL FOR…

1

2

3

- ☐ MEDITATION
- ☐ YOGA
- ☐ EXERCISE
- ☐ ACKNOWLEDGEMENT
- ☐ AFFIRMATIONS
- ☐ _____

DREAMS FROM LAST NIGHT:

MY BEST 24-HOUR MOMENT:

TODAY, I WILL ACCOMPLISH…

TODAY, I WILL GROW BY…

For more inspiration, go to iamaluminary.com.

Manifestation Mantra:

DATE:

I'M GRATEFUL FOR...

1

2

3

- ☐ MEDITATION
- ☐ YOGA
- ☐ EXERCISE
- ☐ ACKNOWLEDGEMENT
- ☐ AFFIRMATIONS
- ☐ _____

DREAMS FROM LAST NIGHT:

MY BEST 24-HOUR MOMENT:

TODAY, I WILL ACCOMPLISH...

TODAY, I WILL GROW BY...

DATE:

I'M GRATEFUL FOR...

1

2

3

- ☐ MEDITATION
- ☐ YOGA
- ☐ EXERCISE
- ☐ ACKNOWLEDGEMENT
- ☐ AFFIRMATIONS
- ☐ _____

DREAMS FROM LAST NIGHT:

MY BEST 24-HOUR MOMENT:

TODAY, I WILL ACCOMPLISH...

TODAY, I WILL GROW BY...

For more inspiration, go to iamaluminary.com.

Manifestation Mantra:

DATE:

I'M GRATEFUL FOR...

1

2

3

- ☐ MEDITATION
- ☐ YOGA
- ☐ EXERCISE
- ☐ ACKNOWLEDGEMENT
- ☐ AFFIRMATIONS
- ☐ _____

DREAMS FROM LAST NIGHT:

MY BEST 24-HOUR MOMENT:

TODAY, I WILL ACCOMPLISH...

TODAY, I WILL GROW BY...

DATE:

I'M GRATEFUL FOR...

1

2

3

- ☐ MEDITATION
- ☐ YOGA
- ☐ EXERCISE
- ☐ ACKNOWLEDGEMENT
- ☐ AFFIRMATIONS
- ☐ _____

DREAMS FROM LAST NIGHT:

MY BEST 24-HOUR MOMENT:

TODAY, I WILL ACCOMPLISH...

TODAY, I WILL GROW BY...

For more inspiration, go to iamaluminary.com.

Manifestation Mantra:

DATE:

I'M GRATEFUL FOR…

1

2

3

- ☐ MEDITATION
- ☐ YOGA
- ☐ EXERCISE
- ☐ ACKNOWLEDGEMENT
- ☐ AFFIRMATIONS
- ☐ _____

DREAMS FROM LAST NIGHT:

MY BEST 24-HOUR MOMENT:

TODAY, I WILL ACCOMPLISH…

TODAY, I WILL GROW BY…

DATE:

I'M GRATEFUL FOR…

1

2

3

- ☐ MEDITATION
- ☐ YOGA
- ☐ EXERCISE
- ☐ ACKNOWLEDGEMENT
- ☐ AFFIRMATIONS
- ☐ _____

DREAMS FROM LAST NIGHT:

MY BEST 24-HOUR MOMENT:

TODAY, I WILL ACCOMPLISH…

TODAY, I WILL GROW BY…

Manifestation Mantra:

DATE:

I'M GRATEFUL FOR...

1

2

3

- ☐ MEDITATION
- ☐ YOGA
- ☐ EXERCISE
- ☐ ACKNOWLEDGEMENT
- ☐ AFFIRMATIONS
- ☐ _____

DREAMS FROM LAST NIGHT:

MY BEST 24-HOUR MOMENT:

TODAY, I WILL ACCOMPLISH...

TODAY, I WILL GROW BY...

DATE:

I'M GRATEFUL FOR...

1

2

3

- ☐ MEDITATION
- ☐ YOGA
- ☐ EXERCISE
- ☐ ACKNOWLEDGEMENT
- ☐ AFFIRMATIONS
- ☐ _____

DREAMS FROM LAST NIGHT:

MY BEST 24-HOUR MOMENT:

TODAY, I WILL ACCOMPLISH...

TODAY, I WILL GROW BY...

For more inspiration, go to iamaluminary.com.

Manifestation Mantra:

DATE:

I'M GRATEFUL FOR...

1

2

3

- ☐ MEDITATION
- ☐ YOGA
- ☐ EXERCISE
- ☐ ACKNOWLEDGEMENT
- ☐ AFFIRMATIONS
- ☐ _____

DREAMS FROM LAST NIGHT:

MY BEST 24-HOUR MOMENT:

TODAY, I WILL ACCOMPLISH...

TODAY, I WILL GROW BY...

DATE:

I'M GRATEFUL FOR...

1

2

3

- ☐ MEDITATION
- ☐ YOGA
- ☐ EXERCISE
- ☐ ACKNOWLEDGEMENT
- ☐ AFFIRMATIONS
- ☐ _____

DREAMS FROM LAST NIGHT:

MY BEST 24-HOUR MOMENT:

TODAY, I WILL ACCOMPLISH...

TODAY, I WILL GROW BY...

For more inspiration, go to iamaluminary.com.

Manifestation Mantra:

DATE:

I'M GRATEFUL FOR...

1

2

3

- ☐ MEDITATION
- ☐ YOGA
- ☐ EXERCISE
- ☐ ACKNOWLEDGEMENT
- ☐ AFFIRMATIONS
- ☐ _____

DREAMS FROM LAST NIGHT:

MY BEST 24-HOUR MOMENT:

TODAY, I WILL ACCOMPLISH...

TODAY, I WILL GROW BY...

DATE:

I'M GRATEFUL FOR...

1

2

3

- ☐ MEDITATION
- ☐ YOGA
- ☐ EXERCISE
- ☐ ACKNOWLEDGEMENT
- ☐ AFFIRMATIONS
- ☐ _____

DREAMS FROM LAST NIGHT:

MY BEST 24-HOUR MOMENT:

TODAY, I WILL ACCOMPLISH...

TODAY, I WILL GROW BY...

Manifestation Mantra:

DATE:

I'M GRATEFUL FOR...

1

2

3

- ☐ MEDITATION
- ☐ YOGA
- ☐ EXERCISE
- ☐ ACKNOWLEDGEMENT
- ☐ AFFIRMATIONS
- ☐ _____

DREAMS FROM LAST NIGHT:

MY BEST 24-HOUR MOMENT:

TODAY, I WILL ACCOMPLISH...

TODAY, I WILL GROW BY...

DATE:

I'M GRATEFUL FOR...

1

2

3

- ☐ MEDITATION
- ☐ YOGA
- ☐ EXERCISE
- ☐ ACKNOWLEDGEMENT
- ☐ AFFIRMATIONS
- ☐ _____

DREAMS FROM LAST NIGHT:

MY BEST 24-HOUR MOMENT:

TODAY, I WILL ACCOMPLISH...

TODAY, I WILL GROW BY...

For more inspiration, go to iamaluminary.com.

Manifestation Mantra:

DATE:

I'M GRATEFUL FOR...

1

2

3

- ☐ MEDITATION
- ☐ YOGA
- ☐ EXERCISE
- ☐ ACKNOWLEDGEMENT
- ☐ AFFIRMATIONS
- ☐ _____

DREAMS FROM LAST NIGHT:

MY BEST 24-HOUR MOMENT:

TODAY, I WILL ACCOMPLISH...

TODAY, I WILL GROW BY...

DATE:

I'M GRATEFUL FOR...

1

2

3

- ☐ MEDITATION
- ☐ YOGA
- ☐ EXERCISE
- ☐ ACKNOWLEDGEMENT
- ☐ AFFIRMATIONS
- ☐ _____

DREAMS FROM LAST NIGHT:

MY BEST 24-HOUR MOMENT:

TODAY, I WILL ACCOMPLISH...

TODAY, I WILL GROW BY...

For more inspiration, go to iamaluminary.com.

Manifestation Mantra:

DATE:

I'M GRATEFUL FOR…

1

2

3

- ☐ MEDITATION
- ☐ YOGA
- ☐ EXERCISE
- ☐ ACKNOWLEDGEMENT
- ☐ AFFIRMATIONS
- ☐ _____

DREAMS FROM LAST NIGHT:

MY BEST 24-HOUR MOMENT:

TODAY, I WILL ACCOMPLISH…

TODAY, I WILL GROW BY…

DATE:

I'M GRATEFUL FOR…

1

2

3

- ☐ MEDITATION
- ☐ YOGA
- ☐ EXERCISE
- ☐ ACKNOWLEDGEMENT
- ☐ AFFIRMATIONS
- ☐ _____

DREAMS FROM LAST NIGHT:

MY BEST 24-HOUR MOMENT:

TODAY, I WILL ACCOMPLISH…

TODAY, I WILL GROW BY…

Manifestation Mantra:

DATE:

I'M GRATEFUL FOR...

1

2

3

- ☐ MEDITATION
- ☐ YOGA
- ☐ EXERCISE
- ☐ ACKNOWLEDGEMENT
- ☐ AFFIRMATIONS
- ☐ _____

DREAMS FROM LAST NIGHT:

MY BEST 24-HOUR MOMENT:

TODAY, I WILL ACCOMPLISH...

TODAY, I WILL GROW BY...

DATE:

I'M GRATEFUL FOR...

1

2

3

- ☐ MEDITATION
- ☐ YOGA
- ☐ EXERCISE
- ☐ ACKNOWLEDGEMENT
- ☐ AFFIRMATIONS
- ☐ _____

DREAMS FROM LAST NIGHT:

MY BEST 24-HOUR MOMENT:

TODAY, I WILL ACCOMPLISH...

TODAY, I WILL GROW BY...

Manifestation Mantra:

DATE:

I'M GRATEFUL FOR...

1

2

3

- ☐ MEDITATION
- ☐ YOGA
- ☐ EXERCISE
- ☐ ACKNOWLEDGEMENT
- ☐ AFFIRMATIONS
- ☐ _____

DREAMS FROM LAST NIGHT:

MY BEST 24-HOUR MOMENT:

TODAY, I WILL ACCOMPLISH...

TODAY, I WILL GROW BY...

DATE:

I'M GRATEFUL FOR...

1

2

3

- ☐ MEDITATION
- ☐ YOGA
- ☐ EXERCISE
- ☐ ACKNOWLEDGEMENT
- ☐ AFFIRMATIONS
- ☐ _____

DREAMS FROM LAST NIGHT:

MY BEST 24-HOUR MOMENT:

TODAY, I WILL ACCOMPLISH...

TODAY, I WILL GROW BY...

For more inspiration, go to iamaluminary.com.

Manifestation Mantra:

DATE:

I'M GRATEFUL FOR…

1

2

3

- ☐ MEDITATION
- ☐ YOGA
- ☐ EXERCISE
- ☐ ACKNOWLEDGEMENT
- ☐ AFFIRMATIONS
- ☐ _____

DREAMS FROM LAST NIGHT:

MY BEST 24-HOUR MOMENT:

TODAY, I WILL ACCOMPLISH…

TODAY, I WILL GROW BY…

DATE:

I'M GRATEFUL FOR…

1

2

3

- ☐ MEDITATION
- ☐ YOGA
- ☐ EXERCISE
- ☐ ACKNOWLEDGEMENT
- ☐ AFFIRMATIONS
- ☐ _____

DREAMS FROM LAST NIGHT:

MY BEST 24-HOUR MOMENT:

TODAY, I WILL ACCOMPLISH…

TODAY, I WILL GROW BY…

Manifestation Mantra:

DATE:

I'M GRATEFUL FOR...

1

2

3

- ☐ MEDITATION
- ☐ YOGA
- ☐ EXERCISE
- ☐ ACKNOWLEDGEMENT
- ☐ AFFIRMATIONS
- ☐ _____

DREAMS FROM LAST NIGHT:

MY BEST 24-HOUR MOMENT:

TODAY, I WILL ACCOMPLISH...

TODAY, I WILL GROW BY...

DATE:

I'M GRATEFUL FOR...

1

2

3

- ☐ MEDITATION
- ☐ YOGA
- ☐ EXERCISE
- ☐ ACKNOWLEDGEMENT
- ☐ AFFIRMATIONS
- ☐ _____

DREAMS FROM LAST NIGHT:

MY BEST 24-HOUR MOMENT:

TODAY, I WILL ACCOMPLISH...

TODAY, I WILL GROW BY...

For more inspiration, go to iamaluminary.com.

Manifestation Mantra:

DATE:

I'M GRATEFUL FOR...

1

2

3

- ☐ MEDITATION
- ☐ YOGA
- ☐ EXERCISE
- ☐ ACKNOWLEDGEMENT
- ☐ AFFIRMATIONS
- ☐ _____

DREAMS FROM LAST NIGHT:

MY BEST 24-HOUR MOMENT:

TODAY, I WILL ACCOMPLISH...

TODAY, I WILL GROW BY...

DATE:

I'M GRATEFUL FOR...

1

2

3

- ☐ MEDITATION
- ☐ YOGA
- ☐ EXERCISE
- ☐ ACKNOWLEDGEMENT
- ☐ AFFIRMATIONS
- ☐ _____

DREAMS FROM LAST NIGHT:

MY BEST 24-HOUR MOMENT:

TODAY, I WILL ACCOMPLISH...

TODAY, I WILL GROW BY...

Manifestation Mantra:

DATE:

I'M GRATEFUL FOR...

1

2

3

- ☐ MEDITATION
- ☐ YOGA
- ☐ EXERCISE
- ☐ ACKNOWLEDGEMENT
- ☐ AFFIRMATIONS
- ☐ _____

DREAMS FROM LAST NIGHT:

MY BEST 24-HOUR MOMENT:

TODAY, I WILL ACCOMPLISH...

TODAY, I WILL GROW BY...

DATE:

I'M GRATEFUL FOR...

1

2

3

- ☐ MEDITATION
- ☐ YOGA
- ☐ EXERCISE
- ☐ ACKNOWLEDGEMENT
- ☐ AFFIRMATIONS
- ☐ _____

DREAMS FROM LAST NIGHT:

MY BEST 24-HOUR MOMENT:

TODAY, I WILL ACCOMPLISH...

TODAY, I WILL GROW BY...

Manifestation Mantra:

DATE:

I'M GRATEFUL FOR...

1

2

3

- ☐ MEDITATION
- ☐ YOGA
- ☐ EXERCISE
- ☐ ACKNOWLEDGEMENT
- ☐ AFFIRMATIONS
- ☐ _____

DREAMS FROM LAST NIGHT:

MY BEST 24-HOUR MOMENT:

TODAY, I WILL ACCOMPLISH...

TODAY, I WILL GROW BY...

DATE:

I'M GRATEFUL FOR...

1

2

3

- ☐ MEDITATION
- ☐ YOGA
- ☐ EXERCISE
- ☐ ACKNOWLEDGEMENT
- ☐ AFFIRMATIONS
- ☐ _____

DREAMS FROM LAST NIGHT:

MY BEST 24-HOUR MOMENT:

TODAY, I WILL ACCOMPLISH...

TODAY, I WILL GROW BY...

For more inspiration, go to iamaluminary.com.

Manifestation Mantra:

DATE:

I'M GRATEFUL FOR…

1

2

3

- ☐ MEDITATION
- ☐ YOGA
- ☐ EXERCISE
- ☐ ACKNOWLEDGEMENT
- ☐ AFFIRMATIONS
- ☐ _____

DREAMS FROM LAST NIGHT:

MY BEST 24-HOUR MOMENT:

TODAY, I WILL ACCOMPLISH…

TODAY, I WILL GROW BY…

DATE:

I'M GRATEFUL FOR…

1

2

3

- ☐ MEDITATION
- ☐ YOGA
- ☐ EXERCISE
- ☐ ACKNOWLEDGEMENT
- ☐ AFFIRMATIONS
- ☐ _____

DREAMS FROM LAST NIGHT:

MY BEST 24-HOUR MOMENT:

TODAY, I WILL ACCOMPLISH…

TODAY, I WILL GROW BY…

For more inspiration, go to iamaluminary.com.

Manifestation Mantra:

DATE:

I'M GRATEFUL FOR...

1

2

3

- ☐ MEDITATION
- ☐ YOGA
- ☐ EXERCISE
- ☐ ACKNOWLEDGEMENT
- ☐ AFFIRMATIONS
- ☐ _____

DREAMS FROM LAST NIGHT:

MY BEST 24-HOUR MOMENT:

TODAY, I WILL ACCOMPLISH...

TODAY, I WILL GROW BY...

DATE:

I'M GRATEFUL FOR...

1

2

3

- ☐ MEDITATION
- ☐ YOGA
- ☐ EXERCISE
- ☐ ACKNOWLEDGEMENT
- ☐ AFFIRMATIONS
- ☐ _____

DREAMS FROM LAST NIGHT:

MY BEST 24-HOUR MOMENT:

TODAY, I WILL ACCOMPLISH...

TODAY, I WILL GROW BY...

For more inspiration, go to iamaluminary.com.

Manifestation Mantra:

DATE:

I'M GRATEFUL FOR…

1

2

3

- ☐ MEDITATION
- ☐ YOGA
- ☐ EXERCISE
- ☐ ACKNOWLEDGEMENT
- ☐ AFFIRMATIONS
- ☐ _____

DREAMS FROM LAST NIGHT:

MY BEST 24-HOUR MOMENT:

TODAY, I WILL ACCOMPLISH…

TODAY, I WILL GROW BY…

DATE:

I'M GRATEFUL FOR…

1

2

3

- ☐ MEDITATION
- ☐ YOGA
- ☐ EXERCISE
- ☐ ACKNOWLEDGEMENT
- ☐ AFFIRMATIONS
- ☐ _____

DREAMS FROM LAST NIGHT:

MY BEST 24-HOUR MOMENT:

TODAY, I WILL ACCOMPLISH…

TODAY, I WILL GROW BY…

For more inspiration, go to iamaluminary.com.

Manifestation Mantra:

DATE:

I'M GRATEFUL FOR…

1

2

3

- ☐ MEDITATION
- ☐ YOGA
- ☐ EXERCISE
- ☐ ACKNOWLEDGEMENT
- ☐ AFFIRMATIONS
- ☐ _____

DREAMS FROM LAST NIGHT:

MY BEST 24-HOUR MOMENT:

TODAY, I WILL ACCOMPLISH…

TODAY, I WILL GROW BY…

DATE:

I'M GRATEFUL FOR…

1

2

3

- ☐ MEDITATION
- ☐ YOGA
- ☐ EXERCISE
- ☐ ACKNOWLEDGEMENT
- ☐ AFFIRMATIONS
- ☐ _____

DREAMS FROM LAST NIGHT:

MY BEST 24-HOUR MOMENT:

TODAY, I WILL ACCOMPLISH…

TODAY, I WILL GROW BY…

Manifestation Mantra:

DATE:

I'M GRATEFUL FOR...

1

2

3

- ☐ MEDITATION
- ☐ YOGA
- ☐ EXERCISE
- ☐ ACKNOWLEDGEMENT
- ☐ AFFIRMATIONS
- ☐ _____

DREAMS FROM LAST NIGHT:

MY BEST 24-HOUR MOMENT:

TODAY, I WILL ACCOMPLISH...

TODAY, I WILL GROW BY...

DATE:

I'M GRATEFUL FOR...

1

2

3

- ☐ MEDITATION
- ☐ YOGA
- ☐ EXERCISE
- ☐ ACKNOWLEDGEMENT
- ☐ AFFIRMATIONS
- ☐ _____

DREAMS FROM LAST NIGHT:

MY BEST 24-HOUR MOMENT:

TODAY, I WILL ACCOMPLISH...

TODAY, I WILL GROW BY...

For more inspiration, go to iamaluminary.com.

Manifestation Mantra:

DATE:

I'M GRATEFUL FOR...

1

2

3

- ☐ MEDITATION
- ☐ YOGA
- ☐ EXERCISE
- ☐ ACKNOWLEDGEMENT
- ☐ AFFIRMATIONS
- ☐ _____

DREAMS FROM LAST NIGHT:

MY BEST 24-HOUR MOMENT:

TODAY, I WILL ACCOMPLISH...

TODAY, I WILL GROW BY...

DATE:

I'M GRATEFUL FOR...

1

2

3

- ☐ MEDITATION
- ☐ YOGA
- ☐ EXERCISE
- ☐ ACKNOWLEDGEMENT
- ☐ AFFIRMATIONS
- ☐ _____

DREAMS FROM LAST NIGHT:

MY BEST 24-HOUR MOMENT:

TODAY, I WILL ACCOMPLISH...

TODAY, I WILL GROW BY...

For more inspiration, go to iamaluminary.com.

Manifestation Mantra:

DATE:

I'M GRATEFUL FOR...

1

2

3

- ☐ MEDITATION
- ☐ YOGA
- ☐ EXERCISE
- ☐ ACKNOWLEDGEMENT
- ☐ AFFIRMATIONS
- ☐ _____

DREAMS FROM LAST NIGHT:

MY BEST 24-HOUR MOMENT:

TODAY, I WILL ACCOMPLISH...

TODAY, I WILL GROW BY...

DATE:

I'M GRATEFUL FOR...

1

2

3

- ☐ MEDITATION
- ☐ YOGA
- ☐ EXERCISE
- ☐ ACKNOWLEDGEMENT
- ☐ AFFIRMATIONS
- ☐ _____

DREAMS FROM LAST NIGHT:

MY BEST 24-HOUR MOMENT:

TODAY, I WILL ACCOMPLISH...

TODAY, I WILL GROW BY...

For more inspiration, go to iamaluminary.com.

Manifestation Mantra:

DATE:

I'M GRATEFUL FOR...

1

2

3

- ☐ MEDITATION
- ☐ YOGA
- ☐ EXERCISE
- ☐ ACKNOWLEDGEMENT
- ☐ AFFIRMATIONS
- ☐ _____

DREAMS FROM LAST NIGHT:

MY BEST 24-HOUR MOMENT:

TODAY, I WILL ACCOMPLISH...

TODAY, I WILL GROW BY...

DATE:

I'M GRATEFUL FOR...

1

2

3

- ☐ MEDITATION
- ☐ YOGA
- ☐ EXERCISE
- ☐ ACKNOWLEDGEMENT
- ☐ AFFIRMATIONS
- ☐ _____

DREAMS FROM LAST NIGHT:

MY BEST 24-HOUR MOMENT:

TODAY, I WILL ACCOMPLISH...

TODAY, I WILL GROW BY...

For more inspiration, go to iamaluminary.com.

Manifestation Mantra:

DATE:

I'M GRATEFUL FOR...

1

2

3

- ☐ MEDITATION
- ☐ YOGA
- ☐ EXERCISE
- ☐ ACKNOWLEDGEMENT
- ☐ AFFIRMATIONS
- ☐ _____

DREAMS FROM LAST NIGHT:

MY BEST 24-HOUR MOMENT:

TODAY, I WILL ACCOMPLISH...

TODAY, I WILL GROW BY...

DATE:

I'M GRATEFUL FOR...

1

2

3

- ☐ MEDITATION
- ☐ YOGA
- ☐ EXERCISE
- ☐ ACKNOWLEDGEMENT
- ☐ AFFIRMATIONS
- ☐ _____

DREAMS FROM LAST NIGHT:

MY BEST 24-HOUR MOMENT:

TODAY, I WILL ACCOMPLISH...

TODAY, I WILL GROW BY...

For more inspiration, go to iamaluminary.com.

Manifestation Mantra:

DATE:

I'M GRATEFUL FOR...

1

2

3

- ☐ MEDITATION
- ☐ YOGA
- ☐ EXERCISE
- ☐ ACKNOWLEDGEMENT
- ☐ AFFIRMATIONS
- ☐ _____

DREAMS FROM LAST NIGHT:

MY BEST 24-HOUR MOMENT:

TODAY, I WILL ACCOMPLISH...

TODAY, I WILL GROW BY...

DATE:

I'M GRATEFUL FOR...

1

2

3

- ☐ MEDITATION
- ☐ YOGA
- ☐ EXERCISE
- ☐ ACKNOWLEDGEMENT
- ☐ AFFIRMATIONS
- ☐ _____

DREAMS FROM LAST NIGHT:

MY BEST 24-HOUR MOMENT:

TODAY, I WILL ACCOMPLISH...

TODAY, I WILL GROW BY...

Manifestation Mantra:

DATE:

I'M GRATEFUL FOR...

1

2

3

- ☐ MEDITATION
- ☐ YOGA
- ☐ EXERCISE
- ☐ ACKNOWLEDGEMENT
- ☐ AFFIRMATIONS
- ☐ _____

DREAMS FROM LAST NIGHT:

MY BEST 24-HOUR MOMENT:

TODAY, I WILL ACCOMPLISH...

TODAY, I WILL GROW BY...

DATE:

I'M GRATEFUL FOR...

1

2

3

- ☐ MEDITATION
- ☐ YOGA
- ☐ EXERCISE
- ☐ ACKNOWLEDGEMENT
- ☐ AFFIRMATIONS
- ☐ _____

DREAMS FROM LAST NIGHT:

MY BEST 24-HOUR MOMENT:

TODAY, I WILL ACCOMPLISH...

TODAY, I WILL GROW BY...

For more inspiration, go to iamaluminary.com.

Manifestation Mantra:

DATE:

I'M GRATEFUL FOR...

1

2

3

- ☐ MEDITATION
- ☐ YOGA
- ☐ EXERCISE
- ☐ ACKNOWLEDGEMENT
- ☐ AFFIRMATIONS
- ☐ _____

DREAMS FROM LAST NIGHT:

MY BEST 24-HOUR MOMENT:

TODAY, I WILL ACCOMPLISH...

TODAY, I WILL GROW BY...

DATE:

I'M GRATEFUL FOR...

1

2

3

- ☐ MEDITATION
- ☐ YOGA
- ☐ EXERCISE
- ☐ ACKNOWLEDGEMENT
- ☐ AFFIRMATIONS
- ☐ _____

DREAMS FROM LAST NIGHT:

MY BEST 24-HOUR MOMENT:

TODAY, I WILL ACCOMPLISH...

TODAY, I WILL GROW BY...

For more inspiration, go to iamaluminary.com.

Manifestation Mantra:

DATE:

I'M GRATEFUL FOR...

1

2

3

- ☐ MEDITATION
- ☐ YOGA
- ☐ EXERCISE
- ☐ ACKNOWLEDGEMENT
- ☐ AFFIRMATIONS
- ☐ _____

DREAMS FROM LAST NIGHT:

MY BEST 24-HOUR MOMENT:

TODAY, I WILL ACCOMPLISH...

TODAY, I WILL GROW BY...

DATE:

I'M GRATEFUL FOR...

1

2

3

- ☐ MEDITATION
- ☐ YOGA
- ☐ EXERCISE
- ☐ ACKNOWLEDGEMENT
- ☐ AFFIRMATIONS
- ☐ _____

DREAMS FROM LAST NIGHT:

MY BEST 24-HOUR MOMENT:

TODAY, I WILL ACCOMPLISH...

TODAY, I WILL GROW BY...

For more inspiration, go to iamaluminary.com.

Manifestation Mantra:

DATE:

I'M GRATEFUL FOR…

1

2

3

- ☐ MEDITATION
- ☐ YOGA
- ☐ EXERCISE
- ☐ ACKNOWLEDGEMENT
- ☐ AFFIRMATIONS
- ☐ _____

DREAMS FROM LAST NIGHT:

MY BEST 24-HOUR MOMENT:

TODAY, I WILL ACCOMPLISH…

TODAY, I WILL GROW BY…

DATE:

I'M GRATEFUL FOR…

1

2

3

- ☐ MEDITATION
- ☐ YOGA
- ☐ EXERCISE
- ☐ ACKNOWLEDGEMENT
- ☐ AFFIRMATIONS
- ☐ _____

DREAMS FROM LAST NIGHT:

MY BEST 24-HOUR MOMENT:

TODAY, I WILL ACCOMPLISH…

TODAY, I WILL GROW BY…

Manifestation Mantra:

DATE:

I'M GRATEFUL FOR…

1

2

3

- ☐ MEDITATION
- ☐ YOGA
- ☐ EXERCISE
- ☐ ACKNOWLEDGEMENT
- ☐ AFFIRMATIONS
- ☐ _____

DREAMS FROM LAST NIGHT:

MY BEST 24-HOUR MOMENT:

TODAY, I WILL ACCOMPLISH…

TODAY, I WILL GROW BY…

DATE:

I'M GRATEFUL FOR…

1

2

3

- ☐ MEDITATION
- ☐ YOGA
- ☐ EXERCISE
- ☐ ACKNOWLEDGEMENT
- ☐ AFFIRMATIONS
- ☐ _____

DREAMS FROM LAST NIGHT:

MY BEST 24-HOUR MOMENT:

TODAY, I WILL ACCOMPLISH…

TODAY, I WILL GROW BY…

Manifestation Mantra:

DATE:

I'M GRATEFUL FOR...

1

2

3

- ☐ MEDITATION
- ☐ YOGA
- ☐ EXERCISE
- ☐ ACKNOWLEDGEMENT
- ☐ AFFIRMATIONS
- ☐ _____

DREAMS FROM LAST NIGHT:

MY BEST 24-HOUR MOMENT:

TODAY, I WILL ACCOMPLISH...

TODAY, I WILL GROW BY...

DATE:

I'M GRATEFUL FOR...

1

2

3

- ☐ MEDITATION
- ☐ YOGA
- ☐ EXERCISE
- ☐ ACKNOWLEDGEMENT
- ☐ AFFIRMATIONS
- ☐ _____

DREAMS FROM LAST NIGHT:

MY BEST 24-HOUR MOMENT:

TODAY, I WILL ACCOMPLISH...

TODAY, I WILL GROW BY...

Manifestation Mantra:

DATE:

I'M GRATEFUL FOR...

1

2

3

- ☐ MEDITATION
- ☐ YOGA
- ☐ EXERCISE
- ☐ ACKNOWLEDGEMENT
- ☐ AFFIRMATIONS
- ☐ _____

DREAMS FROM LAST NIGHT:

MY BEST 24-HOUR MOMENT:

TODAY, I WILL ACCOMPLISH...

TODAY, I WILL GROW BY...

DATE:

I'M GRATEFUL FOR...

1

2

3

- ☐ MEDITATION
- ☐ YOGA
- ☐ EXERCISE
- ☐ ACKNOWLEDGEMENT
- ☐ AFFIRMATIONS
- ☐ _____

DREAMS FROM LAST NIGHT:

MY BEST 24-HOUR MOMENT:

TODAY, I WILL ACCOMPLISH...

TODAY, I WILL GROW BY...

For more inspiration, go to iamaluminary.com.

Manifestation Mantra:

DATE:

I'M GRATEFUL FOR...

1

2

3

- ☐ MEDITATION
- ☐ YOGA
- ☐ EXERCISE
- ☐ ACKNOWLEDGEMENT
- ☐ AFFIRMATIONS
- ☐ _____

DREAMS FROM LAST NIGHT:

MY BEST 24-HOUR MOMENT:

TODAY, I WILL ACCOMPLISH...

TODAY, I WILL GROW BY...

DATE:

I'M GRATEFUL FOR...

1

2

3

- ☐ MEDITATION
- ☐ YOGA
- ☐ EXERCISE
- ☐ ACKNOWLEDGEMENT
- ☐ AFFIRMATIONS
- ☐ _____

DREAMS FROM LAST NIGHT:

MY BEST 24-HOUR MOMENT:

TODAY, I WILL ACCOMPLISH...

TODAY, I WILL GROW BY...

Manifestation Mantra:

DATE:

I'M GRATEFUL FOR...

1

2

3

- ☐ MEDITATION
- ☐ YOGA
- ☐ EXERCISE
- ☐ ACKNOWLEDGEMENT
- ☐ AFFIRMATIONS
- ☐ _____

DREAMS FROM LAST NIGHT:

MY BEST 24-HOUR MOMENT:

TODAY, I WILL ACCOMPLISH...

TODAY, I WILL GROW BY...

DATE:

I'M GRATEFUL FOR...

1

2

3

- ☐ MEDITATION
- ☐ YOGA
- ☐ EXERCISE
- ☐ ACKNOWLEDGEMENT
- ☐ AFFIRMATIONS
- ☐ _____

DREAMS FROM LAST NIGHT:

MY BEST 24-HOUR MOMENT:

TODAY, I WILL ACCOMPLISH...

TODAY, I WILL GROW BY...

Manifestation Mantra:

DATE:

I'M GRATEFUL FOR...

1

2

3

- ☐ MEDITATION
- ☐ YOGA
- ☐ EXERCISE
- ☐ ACKNOWLEDGEMENT
- ☐ AFFIRMATIONS
- ☐ _____

DREAMS FROM LAST NIGHT:

MY BEST 24-HOUR MOMENT:

TODAY, I WILL ACCOMPLISH...

TODAY, I WILL GROW BY...

DATE:

I'M GRATEFUL FOR...

1

2

3

- ☐ MEDITATION
- ☐ YOGA
- ☐ EXERCISE
- ☐ ACKNOWLEDGEMENT
- ☐ AFFIRMATIONS
- ☐ _____

DREAMS FROM LAST NIGHT:

MY BEST 24-HOUR MOMENT:

TODAY, I WILL ACCOMPLISH...

TODAY, I WILL GROW BY...

Manifestation Mantra:

DATE:

I'M GRATEFUL FOR…

1

2

3

- ☐ MEDITATION
- ☐ YOGA
- ☐ EXERCISE
- ☐ ACKNOWLEDGEMENT
- ☐ AFFIRMATIONS
- ☐ _____

DREAMS FROM LAST NIGHT:

MY BEST 24-HOUR MOMENT:

TODAY, I WILL ACCOMPLISH…

TODAY, I WILL GROW BY…

DATE:

I'M GRATEFUL FOR…

1

2

3

- ☐ MEDITATION
- ☐ YOGA
- ☐ EXERCISE
- ☐ ACKNOWLEDGEMENT
- ☐ AFFIRMATIONS
- ☐ _____

DREAMS FROM LAST NIGHT:

MY BEST 24-HOUR MOMENT:

TODAY, I WILL ACCOMPLISH…

TODAY, I WILL GROW BY…

For more inspiration, go to iamaluminary.com.

Manifestation Mantra:

DATE:

I'M GRATEFUL FOR...

1

2

3

- ☐ MEDITATION
- ☐ YOGA
- ☐ EXERCISE
- ☐ ACKNOWLEDGEMENT
- ☐ AFFIRMATIONS
- ☐ _____

DREAMS FROM LAST NIGHT:

MY BEST 24-HOUR MOMENT:

TODAY, I WILL ACCOMPLISH...

TODAY, I WILL GROW BY...

DATE:

I'M GRATEFUL FOR...

1

2

3

- ☐ MEDITATION
- ☐ YOGA
- ☐ EXERCISE
- ☐ ACKNOWLEDGEMENT
- ☐ AFFIRMATIONS
- ☐ _____

DREAMS FROM LAST NIGHT:

MY BEST 24-HOUR MOMENT:

TODAY, I WILL ACCOMPLISH...

TODAY, I WILL GROW BY...

For more inspiration, go to iamaluminary.com.

Manifestation Mantra:

DATE:

I'M GRATEFUL FOR...

1

2

3

- ☐ MEDITATION
- ☐ YOGA
- ☐ EXERCISE
- ☐ ACKNOWLEDGEMENT
- ☐ AFFIRMATIONS
- ☐ _____

DREAMS FROM LAST NIGHT:

MY BEST 24-HOUR MOMENT:

TODAY, I WILL ACCOMPLISH...

TODAY, I WILL GROW BY...

DATE:

I'M GRATEFUL FOR...

1

2

3

- ☐ MEDITATION
- ☐ YOGA
- ☐ EXERCISE
- ☐ ACKNOWLEDGEMENT
- ☐ AFFIRMATIONS
- ☐ _____

DREAMS FROM LAST NIGHT:

MY BEST 24-HOUR MOMENT:

TODAY, I WILL ACCOMPLISH...

TODAY, I WILL GROW BY...

Manifestation Mantra:

DATE:

I'M GRATEFUL FOR...

1

2

3

☐ MEDITATION
☐ YOGA
☐ EXERCISE
☐ ACKNOWLEDGEMENT
☐ AFFIRMATIONS
☐ _____

DREAMS FROM LAST NIGHT:

MY BEST 24-HOUR MOMENT:

TODAY, I WILL ACCOMPLISH...

TODAY, I WILL GROW BY...

DATE:

I'M GRATEFUL FOR...

1

2

3

☐ MEDITATION
☐ YOGA
☐ EXERCISE
☐ ACKNOWLEDGEMENT
☐ AFFIRMATIONS
☐ _____

DREAMS FROM LAST NIGHT:

MY BEST 24-HOUR MOMENT:

TODAY, I WILL ACCOMPLISH...

TODAY, I WILL GROW BY...

For more inspiration, go to iamaluminary.com.

Manifestation Mantra:

DATE:

I'M GRATEFUL FOR…

1

2

3

- ☐ MEDITATION
- ☐ YOGA
- ☐ EXERCISE
- ☐ ACKNOWLEDGEMENT
- ☐ AFFIRMATIONS
- ☐ _____

DREAMS FROM LAST NIGHT:

MY BEST 24-HOUR MOMENT:

TODAY, I WILL ACCOMPLISH…

TODAY, I WILL GROW BY…

DATE:

I'M GRATEFUL FOR…

1

2

3

- ☐ MEDITATION
- ☐ YOGA
- ☐ EXERCISE
- ☐ ACKNOWLEDGEMENT
- ☐ AFFIRMATIONS
- ☐ _____

DREAMS FROM LAST NIGHT:

MY BEST 24-HOUR MOMENT:

TODAY, I WILL ACCOMPLISH…

TODAY, I WILL GROW BY…

For more inspiration, go to iamaluminary.com.

Manifestation Mantra:

DATE:

I'M GRATEFUL FOR...

1

2

3

- ☐ MEDITATION
- ☐ YOGA
- ☐ EXERCISE
- ☐ ACKNOWLEDGEMENT
- ☐ AFFIRMATIONS
- ☐ _____

DREAMS FROM LAST NIGHT:

MY BEST 24-HOUR MOMENT:

TODAY, I WILL ACCOMPLISH...

TODAY, I WILL GROW BY...

DATE:

I'M GRATEFUL FOR...

1

2

3

- ☐ MEDITATION
- ☐ YOGA
- ☐ EXERCISE
- ☐ ACKNOWLEDGEMENT
- ☐ AFFIRMATIONS
- ☐ _____

DREAMS FROM LAST NIGHT:

MY BEST 24-HOUR MOMENT:

TODAY, I WILL ACCOMPLISH...

TODAY, I WILL GROW BY...

Manifestation Mantra:

DATE:

I'M GRATEFUL FOR...

1

2

3

- ☐ MEDITATION
- ☐ YOGA
- ☐ EXERCISE
- ☐ ACKNOWLEDGEMENT
- ☐ AFFIRMATIONS
- ☐ _____

DREAMS FROM LAST NIGHT:

MY BEST 24-HOUR MOMENT:

TODAY, I WILL ACCOMPLISH...

TODAY, I WILL GROW BY...

DATE:

I'M GRATEFUL FOR...

1

2

3

- ☐ MEDITATION
- ☐ YOGA
- ☐ EXERCISE
- ☐ ACKNOWLEDGEMENT
- ☐ AFFIRMATIONS
- ☐ _____

DREAMS FROM LAST NIGHT:

MY BEST 24-HOUR MOMENT:

TODAY, I WILL ACCOMPLISH...

TODAY, I WILL GROW BY...

For more inspiration, go to iamaluminary.com

Manifestation Mantra:

DATE:

I'M GRATEFUL FOR...

1

2

3

- ☐ MEDITATION
- ☐ YOGA
- ☐ EXERCISE
- ☐ ACKNOWLEDGEMENT
- ☐ AFFIRMATIONS
- ☐ _____

DREAMS FROM LAST NIGHT:

MY BEST 24-HOUR MOMENT:

TODAY, I WILL ACCOMPLISH...

TODAY, I WILL GROW BY...

DATE:

I'M GRATEFUL FOR...

1

2

3

- ☐ MEDITATION
- ☐ YOGA
- ☐ EXERCISE
- ☐ ACKNOWLEDGEMENT
- ☐ AFFIRMATIONS
- ☐ _____

DREAMS FROM LAST NIGHT:

MY BEST 24-HOUR MOMENT:

TODAY, I WILL ACCOMPLISH...

TODAY, I WILL GROW BY...

For more inspiration, go to iamaluminary.com.

Manifestation Mantra:

DATE:

I'M GRATEFUL FOR...

1

2

3

- ☐ MEDITATION
- ☐ YOGA
- ☐ EXERCISE
- ☐ ACKNOWLEDGEMENT
- ☐ AFFIRMATIONS
- ☐ _____

DREAMS FROM LAST NIGHT:

MY BEST 24-HOUR MOMENT:

TODAY, I WILL ACCOMPLISH...

TODAY, I WILL GROW BY...

DATE:

I'M GRATEFUL FOR...

1

2

3

- ☐ MEDITATION
- ☐ YOGA
- ☐ EXERCISE
- ☐ ACKNOWLEDGEMENT
- ☐ AFFIRMATIONS
- ☐ _____

DREAMS FROM LAST NIGHT:

MY BEST 24-HOUR MOMENT:

TODAY, I WILL ACCOMPLISH...

TODAY, I WILL GROW BY...

For more inspiration, go to iamaluminary.com.

Manifestation Mantra:

DATE:

I'M GRATEFUL FOR...

1

2

3

- ☐ MEDITATION
- ☐ YOGA
- ☐ EXERCISE
- ☐ ACKNOWLEDGEMENT
- ☐ AFFIRMATIONS
- ☐ _____

DREAMS FROM LAST NIGHT:

MY BEST 24-HOUR MOMENT:

TODAY, I WILL ACCOMPLISH...

TODAY, I WILL GROW BY...

DATE:

I'M GRATEFUL FOR...

1

2

3

- ☐ MEDITATION
- ☐ YOGA
- ☐ EXERCISE
- ☐ ACKNOWLEDGEMENT
- ☐ AFFIRMATIONS
- ☐ _____

DREAMS FROM LAST NIGHT:

MY BEST 24-HOUR MOMENT:

TODAY, I WILL ACCOMPLISH...

TODAY, I WILL GROW BY...

Manifestation Mantra:

DATE:

I'M GRATEFUL FOR…

1

2

3

- ☐ MEDITATION
- ☐ YOGA
- ☐ EXERCISE
- ☐ ACKNOWLEDGEMENT
- ☐ AFFIRMATIONS
- ☐ _____

DREAMS FROM LAST NIGHT:

MY BEST 24-HOUR MOMENT:

TODAY, I WILL ACCOMPLISH…

TODAY, I WILL GROW BY…

DATE:

I'M GRATEFUL FOR…

1

2

3

- ☐ MEDITATION
- ☐ YOGA
- ☐ EXERCISE
- ☐ ACKNOWLEDGEMENT
- ☐ AFFIRMATIONS
- ☐ _____

DREAMS FROM LAST NIGHT:

MY BEST 24-HOUR MOMENT:

TODAY, I WILL ACCOMPLISH…

TODAY, I WILL GROW BY…

For more inspiration, go to iamaluminary.com.

Manifestation Mantra:

DATE:

I'M GRATEFUL FOR…

1

2

3

- ☐ MEDITATION
- ☐ YOGA
- ☐ EXERCISE
- ☐ ACKNOWLEDGEMENT
- ☐ AFFIRMATIONS
- ☐ _____

DREAMS FROM LAST NIGHT:

MY BEST 24-HOUR MOMENT:

TODAY, I WILL ACCOMPLISH…

TODAY, I WILL GROW BY…

DATE:

I'M GRATEFUL FOR…

1

2

3

- ☐ MEDITATION
- ☐ YOGA
- ☐ EXERCISE
- ☐ ACKNOWLEDGEMENT
- ☐ AFFIRMATIONS
- ☐ _____

DREAMS FROM LAST NIGHT:

MY BEST 24-HOUR MOMENT:

TODAY, I WILL ACCOMPLISH…

TODAY, I WILL GROW BY…

For more inspiration, go to iamaluminary.com.

Manifestation Mantra:

DATE:

I'M GRATEFUL FOR…

1

2

3

- ☐ MEDITATION
- ☐ YOGA
- ☐ EXERCISE
- ☐ ACKNOWLEDGEMENT
- ☐ AFFIRMATIONS
- ☐ _____

DREAMS FROM LAST NIGHT:

MY BEST 24-HOUR MOMENT:

TODAY, I WILL ACCOMPLISH…

TODAY, I WILL GROW BY…

DATE:

I'M GRATEFUL FOR…

1

2

3

- ☐ MEDITATION
- ☐ YOGA
- ☐ EXERCISE
- ☐ ACKNOWLEDGEMENT
- ☐ AFFIRMATIONS
- ☐ _____

DREAMS FROM LAST NIGHT:

MY BEST 24-HOUR MOMENT:

TODAY, I WILL ACCOMPLISH…

TODAY, I WILL GROW BY…

Manifestation Mantra:

DATE:

I'M GRATEFUL FOR...

1

2

3

- ☐ MEDITATION
- ☐ YOGA
- ☐ EXERCISE
- ☐ ACKNOWLEDGEMENT
- ☐ AFFIRMATIONS
- ☐ _____

DREAMS FROM LAST NIGHT:

MY BEST 24-HOUR MOMENT:

TODAY, I WILL ACCOMPLISH...

TODAY, I WILL GROW BY...

DATE:

I'M GRATEFUL FOR...

1

2

3

- ☐ MEDITATION
- ☐ YOGA
- ☐ EXERCISE
- ☐ ACKNOWLEDGEMENT
- ☐ AFFIRMATIONS
- ☐ _____

DREAMS FROM LAST NIGHT:

MY BEST 24-HOUR MOMENT:

TODAY, I WILL ACCOMPLISH...

TODAY, I WILL GROW BY...

Manifestation Mantra:

DATE:

I'M GRATEFUL FOR...

1

2

3

- ☐ MEDITATION
- ☐ YOGA
- ☐ EXERCISE
- ☐ ACKNOWLEDGEMENT
- ☐ AFFIRMATIONS
- ☐ _____

DREAMS FROM LAST NIGHT:

MY BEST 24-HOUR MOMENT:

TODAY, I WILL ACCOMPLISH...

TODAY, I WILL GROW BY...

DATE:

I'M GRATEFUL FOR...

1

2

3

- ☐ MEDITATION
- ☐ YOGA
- ☐ EXERCISE
- ☐ ACKNOWLEDGEMENT
- ☐ AFFIRMATIONS
- ☐ _____

DREAMS FROM LAST NIGHT:

MY BEST 24-HOUR MOMENT:

TODAY, I WILL ACCOMPLISH...

TODAY, I WILL GROW BY...

For more inspiration, go to iamaluminary.com.

Manifestation Mantra:

DATE:

I'M GRATEFUL FOR...

1

2

3

- ☐ MEDITATION
- ☐ YOGA
- ☐ EXERCISE
- ☐ ACKNOWLEDGEMENT
- ☐ AFFIRMATIONS
- ☐ _____

DREAMS FROM LAST NIGHT:

MY BEST 24-HOUR MOMENT:

TODAY, I WILL ACCOMPLISH...

TODAY, I WILL GROW BY...

DATE:

I'M GRATEFUL FOR...

1

2

3

- ☐ MEDITATION
- ☐ YOGA
- ☐ EXERCISE
- ☐ ACKNOWLEDGEMENT
- ☐ AFFIRMATIONS
- ☐ _____

DREAMS FROM LAST NIGHT:

MY BEST 24-HOUR MOMENT:

TODAY, I WILL ACCOMPLISH...

TODAY, I WILL GROW BY...

For more inspiration, go to iamaluminary.com.

Manifestation Mantra:

DATE:

I'M GRATEFUL FOR...

1

2

3

- ☐ MEDITATION
- ☐ YOGA
- ☐ EXERCISE
- ☐ ACKNOWLEDGEMENT
- ☐ AFFIRMATIONS
- ☐ _____

DREAMS FROM LAST NIGHT:

MY BEST 24-HOUR MOMENT:

TODAY, I WILL ACCOMPLISH...

TODAY, I WILL GROW BY...

DATE:

I'M GRATEFUL FOR...

1

2

3

- ☐ MEDITATION
- ☐ YOGA
- ☐ EXERCISE
- ☐ ACKNOWLEDGEMENT
- ☐ AFFIRMATIONS
- ☐ _____

DREAMS FROM LAST NIGHT:

MY BEST 24-HOUR MOMENT:

TODAY, I WILL ACCOMPLISH...

TODAY, I WILL GROW BY...

For more inspiration, go to iamaluminary.com.

Manifestation Mantra:

DATE:

I'M GRATEFUL FOR...

1

2

3

- ☐ MEDITATION
- ☐ YOGA
- ☐ EXERCISE
- ☐ ACKNOWLEDGEMENT
- ☐ AFFIRMATIONS
- ☐ _____

DREAMS FROM LAST NIGHT:

MY BEST 24-HOUR MOMENT:

TODAY, I WILL ACCOMPLISH...

TODAY, I WILL GROW BY...

DATE:

I'M GRATEFUL FOR...

1

2

3

- ☐ MEDITATION
- ☐ YOGA
- ☐ EXERCISE
- ☐ ACKNOWLEDGEMENT
- ☐ AFFIRMATIONS
- ☐ _____

DREAMS FROM LAST NIGHT:

MY BEST 24-HOUR MOMENT:

TODAY, I WILL ACCOMPLISH...

TODAY, I WILL GROW BY...

For more inspiration, go to iamaluminary.com.

Manifestation Mantra:

DATE:

I'M GRATEFUL FOR...

1

2

3

- ☐ MEDITATION
- ☐ YOGA
- ☐ EXERCISE
- ☐ ACKNOWLEDGEMENT
- ☐ AFFIRMATIONS
- ☐ _____

DREAMS FROM LAST NIGHT:

MY BEST 24-HOUR MOMENT:

TODAY, I WILL ACCOMPLISH...

TODAY, I WILL GROW BY...

DATE:

I'M GRATEFUL FOR...

1

2

3

- ☐ MEDITATION
- ☐ YOGA
- ☐ EXERCISE
- ☐ ACKNOWLEDGEMENT
- ☐ AFFIRMATIONS
- ☐ _____

DREAMS FROM LAST NIGHT:

MY BEST 24-HOUR MOMENT:

TODAY, I WILL ACCOMPLISH...

TODAY, I WILL GROW BY...

For more inspiration, go to iamaluminary.com.

Manifestation Mantra:

DATE:

I'M GRATEFUL FOR...

1

2

3

- ☐ MEDITATION
- ☐ YOGA
- ☐ EXERCISE
- ☐ ACKNOWLEDGEMENT
- ☐ AFFIRMATIONS
- ☐ _____

DREAMS FROM LAST NIGHT:

MY BEST 24-HOUR MOMENT:

TODAY, I WILL ACCOMPLISH...

TODAY, I WILL GROW BY...

DATE:

I'M GRATEFUL FOR...

1

2

3

- ☐ MEDITATION
- ☐ YOGA
- ☐ EXERCISE
- ☐ ACKNOWLEDGEMENT
- ☐ AFFIRMATIONS
- ☐ _____

DREAMS FROM LAST NIGHT:

MY BEST 24-HOUR MOMENT:

TODAY, I WILL ACCOMPLISH...

TODAY, I WILL GROW BY...

For more inspiration, go to iamaluminary.com.

Manifestation Mantra:

DATE:

I'M GRATEFUL FOR...

1

2

3

- ☐ MEDITATION
- ☐ YOGA
- ☐ EXERCISE
- ☐ ACKNOWLEDGEMENT
- ☐ AFFIRMATIONS
- ☐ _____

DREAMS FROM LAST NIGHT:

MY BEST 24-HOUR MOMENT:

TODAY, I WILL ACCOMPLISH...

TODAY, I WILL GROW BY...

DATE:

I'M GRATEFUL FOR...

1

2

3

- ☐ MEDITATION
- ☐ YOGA
- ☐ EXERCISE
- ☐ ACKNOWLEDGEMENT
- ☐ AFFIRMATIONS
- ☐ _____

DREAMS FROM LAST NIGHT:

MY BEST 24-HOUR MOMENT:

TODAY, I WILL ACCOMPLISH...

TODAY, I WILL GROW BY...

For more inspiration, go to iamaluminary.com.

Manifestation Mantra:

DATE:

I'M GRATEFUL FOR...

1

2

3

- ☐ MEDITATION
- ☐ YOGA
- ☐ EXERCISE
- ☐ ACKNOWLEDGEMENT
- ☐ AFFIRMATIONS
- ☐ _____

DREAMS FROM LAST NIGHT:

MY BEST 24-HOUR MOMENT:

TODAY, I WILL ACCOMPLISH...

TODAY, I WILL GROW BY...

DATE:

I'M GRATEFUL FOR...

1

2

3

- ☐ MEDITATION
- ☐ YOGA
- ☐ EXERCISE
- ☐ ACKNOWLEDGEMENT
- ☐ AFFIRMATIONS
- ☐ _____

DREAMS FROM LAST NIGHT:

MY BEST 24-HOUR MOMENT:

TODAY, I WILL ACCOMPLISH...

TODAY, I WILL GROW BY...

For more inspiration, go to iamaluminary.com.

Manifestation Mantra:

DATE:

I'M GRATEFUL FOR...

1
2
3

- ☐ MEDITATION
- ☐ YOGA
- ☐ EXERCISE
- ☐ ACKNOWLEDGEMENT
- ☐ AFFIRMATIONS
- ☐ _____

DREAMS FROM LAST NIGHT:

MY BEST 24-HOUR MOMENT:

TODAY, I WILL ACCOMPLISH...

TODAY, I WILL GROW BY...

DATE:

I'M GRATEFUL FOR...

1
2
3

- ☐ MEDITATION
- ☐ YOGA
- ☐ EXERCISE
- ☐ ACKNOWLEDGEMENT
- ☐ AFFIRMATIONS
- ☐ _____

DREAMS FROM LAST NIGHT:

MY BEST 24-HOUR MOMENT:

TODAY, I WILL ACCOMPLISH...

TODAY, I WILL GROW BY...

For more inspiration, go to iamaluminary.com.

Manifestation Mantra:

DATE:

I'M GRATEFUL FOR...

1

2

3

- ☐ MEDITATION
- ☐ YOGA
- ☐ EXERCISE
- ☐ ACKNOWLEDGEMENT
- ☐ AFFIRMATIONS
- ☐ _____

DREAMS FROM LAST NIGHT:

MY BEST 24-HOUR MOMENT:

TODAY, I WILL ACCOMPLISH...

TODAY, I WILL GROW BY...

DATE:

I'M GRATEFUL FOR...

1

2

3

- ☐ MEDITATION
- ☐ YOGA
- ☐ EXERCISE
- ☐ ACKNOWLEDGEMENT
- ☐ AFFIRMATIONS
- ☐ _____

DREAMS FROM LAST NIGHT:

MY BEST 24-HOUR MOMENT:

TODAY, I WILL ACCOMPLISH...

TODAY, I WILL GROW BY...

For more inspiration, go to iamaluminary.com.

Manifestation Mantra:

DATE:

I'M GRATEFUL FOR…

1

2

3

- ☐ MEDITATION
- ☐ YOGA
- ☐ EXERCISE
- ☐ ACKNOWLEDGEMENT
- ☐ AFFIRMATIONS
- ☐ _____

DREAMS FROM LAST NIGHT:

MY BEST 24-HOUR MOMENT:

TODAY, I WILL ACCOMPLISH…

TODAY, I WILL GROW BY…

DATE:

I'M GRATEFUL FOR…

1

2

3

- ☐ MEDITATION
- ☐ YOGA
- ☐ EXERCISE
- ☐ ACKNOWLEDGEMENT
- ☐ AFFIRMATIONS
- ☐ _____

DREAMS FROM LAST NIGHT:

MY BEST 24-HOUR MOMENT:

TODAY, I WILL ACCOMPLISH…

TODAY, I WILL GROW BY…

For more inspiration, go to iamaluminary.com.

Manifestation Mantra:

DATE:

I'M GRATEFUL FOR…

1

2

3

- ☐ MEDITATION
- ☐ YOGA
- ☐ EXERCISE
- ☐ ACKNOWLEDGEMENT
- ☐ AFFIRMATIONS
- ☐ _____

DREAMS FROM LAST NIGHT:

MY BEST 24-HOUR MOMENT:

TODAY, I WILL ACCOMPLISH…

TODAY, I WILL GROW BY…

DATE:

I'M GRATEFUL FOR…

1

2

3

- ☐ MEDITATION
- ☐ YOGA
- ☐ EXERCISE
- ☐ ACKNOWLEDGEMENT
- ☐ AFFIRMATIONS
- ☐ _____

DREAMS FROM LAST NIGHT:

MY BEST 24-HOUR MOMENT:

TODAY, I WILL ACCOMPLISH…

TODAY, I WILL GROW BY…

For more inspiration, go to iamaluminary.com.

Manifestation Mantra:

DATE:

I'M GRATEFUL FOR…

1

2

3

- ☐ MEDITATION
- ☐ YOGA
- ☐ EXERCISE
- ☐ ACKNOWLEDGEMENT
- ☐ AFFIRMATIONS
- ☐ _____

DREAMS FROM LAST NIGHT:

MY BEST 24-HOUR MOMENT:

TODAY, I WILL ACCOMPLISH…

TODAY, I WILL GROW BY…

DATE:

I'M GRATEFUL FOR…

1

2

3

- ☐ MEDITATION
- ☐ YOGA
- ☐ EXERCISE
- ☐ ACKNOWLEDGEMENT
- ☐ AFFIRMATIONS
- ☐ _____

DREAMS FROM LAST NIGHT:

MY BEST 24-HOUR MOMENT:

TODAY, I WILL ACCOMPLISH…

TODAY, I WILL GROW BY…

For more inspiration, go to iamaluminary.com.

Manifestation Mantra:

DATE:

I'M GRATEFUL FOR...

1

2

3

- ☐ MEDITATION
- ☐ YOGA
- ☐ EXERCISE
- ☐ ACKNOWLEDGEMENT
- ☐ AFFIRMATIONS
- ☐ _____

DREAMS FROM LAST NIGHT:

MY BEST 24-HOUR MOMENT:

TODAY, I WILL ACCOMPLISH...

TODAY, I WILL GROW BY...

DATE:

I'M GRATEFUL FOR...

1

2

3

- ☐ MEDITATION
- ☐ YOGA
- ☐ EXERCISE
- ☐ ACKNOWLEDGEMENT
- ☐ AFFIRMATIONS
- ☐ _____

DREAMS FROM LAST NIGHT:

MY BEST 24-HOUR MOMENT:

TODAY, I WILL ACCOMPLISH...

TODAY, I WILL GROW BY...

Manifestation Mantra:

DATE:

I'M GRATEFUL FOR...

1

2

3

- ☐ MEDITATION
- ☐ YOGA
- ☐ EXERCISE
- ☐ ACKNOWLEDGEMENT
- ☐ AFFIRMATIONS
- ☐ _____

DREAMS FROM LAST NIGHT:

MY BEST 24-HOUR MOMENT:

TODAY, I WILL ACCOMPLISH...

TODAY, I WILL GROW BY...

DATE:

I'M GRATEFUL FOR...

1

2

3

- ☐ MEDITATION
- ☐ YOGA
- ☐ EXERCISE
- ☐ ACKNOWLEDGEMENT
- ☐ AFFIRMATIONS
- ☐ _____

DREAMS FROM LAST NIGHT:

MY BEST 24-HOUR MOMENT:

TODAY, I WILL ACCOMPLISH...

TODAY, I WILL GROW BY...

For more inspiration, go to iamaluminary.com.

Manifestation Mantra:

DATE:

I'M GRATEFUL FOR…

1

2

3

- ☐ MEDITATION
- ☐ YOGA
- ☐ EXERCISE
- ☐ ACKNOWLEDGEMENT
- ☐ AFFIRMATIONS
- ☐ _____

DREAMS FROM LAST NIGHT:

MY BEST 24-HOUR MOMENT:

TODAY, I WILL ACCOMPLISH…

TODAY, I WILL GROW BY…

DATE:

I'M GRATEFUL FOR…

1

2

3

- ☐ MEDITATION
- ☐ YOGA
- ☐ EXERCISE
- ☐ ACKNOWLEDGEMENT
- ☐ AFFIRMATIONS
- ☐ _____

DREAMS FROM LAST NIGHT:

MY BEST 24-HOUR MOMENT:

TODAY, I WILL ACCOMPLISH…

TODAY, I WILL GROW BY…

Manifestation Mantra:

DATE:

I'M GRATEFUL FOR...

1

2

3

- ☐ MEDITATION
- ☐ YOGA
- ☐ EXERCISE
- ☐ ACKNOWLEDGEMENT
- ☐ AFFIRMATIONS
- ☐ _____

DREAMS FROM LAST NIGHT:

MY BEST 24-HOUR MOMENT:

TODAY, I WILL ACCOMPLISH...

TODAY, I WILL GROW BY...

DATE:

I'M GRATEFUL FOR...

1

2

3

- ☐ MEDITATION
- ☐ YOGA
- ☐ EXERCISE
- ☐ ACKNOWLEDGEMENT
- ☐ AFFIRMATIONS
- ☐ _____

DREAMS FROM LAST NIGHT:

MY BEST 24-HOUR MOMENT:

TODAY, I WILL ACCOMPLISH...

TODAY, I WILL GROW BY...

For more inspiration, go to iamaluminary.com.

Manifestation Mantra:

DATE:

I'M GRATEFUL FOR…

1

2

3

- ☐ MEDITATION
- ☐ YOGA
- ☐ EXERCISE
- ☐ ACKNOWLEDGEMENT
- ☐ AFFIRMATIONS
- ☐ _____

DREAMS FROM LAST NIGHT:

MY BEST 24-HOUR MOMENT:

TODAY, I WILL ACCOMPLISH…

TODAY, I WILL GROW BY…

DATE:

I'M GRATEFUL FOR…

1

2

3

- ☐ MEDITATION
- ☐ YOGA
- ☐ EXERCISE
- ☐ ACKNOWLEDGEMENT
- ☐ AFFIRMATIONS
- ☐ _____

DREAMS FROM LAST NIGHT:

MY BEST 24-HOUR MOMENT:

TODAY, I WILL ACCOMPLISH…

TODAY, I WILL GROW BY…

For more inspiration, go to iamaluminary.com.

Manifestation Mantra:

DATE:

I'M GRATEFUL FOR...

1

2

3

- ☐ MEDITATION
- ☐ YOGA
- ☐ EXERCISE
- ☐ ACKNOWLEDGEMENT
- ☐ AFFIRMATIONS
- ☐ _____

DREAMS FROM LAST NIGHT:

MY BEST 24-HOUR MOMENT:

TODAY, I WILL ACCOMPLISH...

TODAY, I WILL GROW BY...

DATE:

I'M GRATEFUL FOR...

1

2

3

- ☐ MEDITATION
- ☐ YOGA
- ☐ EXERCISE
- ☐ ACKNOWLEDGEMENT
- ☐ AFFIRMATIONS
- ☐ _____

DREAMS FROM LAST NIGHT:

MY BEST 24-HOUR MOMENT:

TODAY, I WILL ACCOMPLISH...

TODAY, I WILL GROW BY...

Manifestation Mantra:

DATE:

I'M GRATEFUL FOR...

1

2

3

- ☐ MEDITATION
- ☐ YOGA
- ☐ EXERCISE
- ☐ ACKNOWLEDGEMENT
- ☐ AFFIRMATIONS
- ☐ _____

DREAMS FROM LAST NIGHT:

MY BEST 24-HOUR MOMENT:

TODAY, I WILL ACCOMPLISH...

TODAY, I WILL GROW BY...

DATE:

I'M GRATEFUL FOR...

1

2

3

- ☐ MEDITATION
- ☐ YOGA
- ☐ EXERCISE
- ☐ ACKNOWLEDGEMENT
- ☐ AFFIRMATIONS
- ☐ _____

DREAMS FROM LAST NIGHT:

MY BEST 24-HOUR MOMENT:

TODAY, I WILL ACCOMPLISH...

TODAY, I WILL GROW BY...

For more inspiration, go to iamaluminary.com.

Manifestation Mantra:

DATE:

I'M GRATEFUL FOR...

1

2

3

- ☐ MEDITATION
- ☐ YOGA
- ☐ EXERCISE
- ☐ ACKNOWLEDGEMENT
- ☐ AFFIRMATIONS
- ☐ _____

DREAMS FROM LAST NIGHT:

MY BEST 24-HOUR MOMENT:

TODAY, I WILL ACCOMPLISH...

TODAY, I WILL GROW BY...

DATE:

I'M GRATEFUL FOR...

1

2

3

- ☐ MEDITATION
- ☐ YOGA
- ☐ EXERCISE
- ☐ ACKNOWLEDGEMENT
- ☐ AFFIRMATIONS
- ☐ _____

DREAMS FROM LAST NIGHT:

MY BEST 24-HOUR MOMENT:

TODAY, I WILL ACCOMPLISH...

TODAY, I WILL GROW BY...

For more inspiration, go to iamaluminary.com.

Manifestation Mantra:

DATE:

I'M GRATEFUL FOR…

1

2

3

- ☐ MEDITATION
- ☐ YOGA
- ☐ EXERCISE
- ☐ ACKNOWLEDGEMENT
- ☐ AFFIRMATIONS
- ☐ _____

DREAMS FROM LAST NIGHT:

MY BEST 24-HOUR MOMENT:

TODAY, I WILL ACCOMPLISH…

TODAY, I WILL GROW BY…

DATE:

I'M GRATEFUL FOR…

1

2

3

- ☐ MEDITATION
- ☐ YOGA
- ☐ EXERCISE
- ☐ ACKNOWLEDGEMENT
- ☐ AFFIRMATIONS
- ☐ _____

DREAMS FROM LAST NIGHT:

MY BEST 24-HOUR MOMENT:

TODAY, I WILL ACCOMPLISH…

TODAY, I WILL GROW BY…

For more inspiration, go to iamaluminary.com.

Manifestation Mantra:

DATE:

I'M GRATEFUL FOR...

1

2

3

- ☐ MEDITATION
- ☐ YOGA
- ☐ EXERCISE
- ☐ ACKNOWLEDGEMENT
- ☐ AFFIRMATIONS
- ☐ _____

DREAMS FROM LAST NIGHT:

MY BEST 24-HOUR MOMENT:

TODAY, I WILL ACCOMPLISH...

TODAY, I WILL GROW BY...

DATE:

I'M GRATEFUL FOR...

1

2

3

- ☐ MEDITATION
- ☐ YOGA
- ☐ EXERCISE
- ☐ ACKNOWLEDGEMENT
- ☐ AFFIRMATIONS
- ☐ _____

DREAMS FROM LAST NIGHT:

MY BEST 24-HOUR MOMENT:

TODAY, I WILL ACCOMPLISH...

TODAY, I WILL GROW BY...

Manifestation Mantra:

DATE:

I'M GRATEFUL FOR...

1

2

3

- ☐ MEDITATION
- ☐ YOGA
- ☐ EXERCISE
- ☐ ACKNOWLEDGEMENT
- ☐ AFFIRMATIONS
- ☐ _____

DREAMS FROM LAST NIGHT:

MY BEST 24-HOUR MOMENT:

TODAY, I WILL ACCOMPLISH...

TODAY, I WILL GROW BY...

DATE:

I'M GRATEFUL FOR...

1

2

3

- ☐ MEDITATION
- ☐ YOGA
- ☐ EXERCISE
- ☐ ACKNOWLEDGEMENT
- ☐ AFFIRMATIONS
- ☐ _____

DREAMS FROM LAST NIGHT:

MY BEST 24-HOUR MOMENT:

TODAY, I WILL ACCOMPLISH...

TODAY, I WILL GROW BY...

For more inspiration, go to iamaluminary.com.

Manifestation Mantra:

DATE:

I'M GRATEFUL FOR...

1

2

3

- ☐ MEDITATION
- ☐ YOGA
- ☐ EXERCISE
- ☐ ACKNOWLEDGEMENT
- ☐ AFFIRMATIONS
- ☐ _____

DREAMS FROM LAST NIGHT:

MY BEST 24-HOUR MOMENT:

TODAY, I WILL ACCOMPLISH...

TODAY, I WILL GROW BY...

DATE:

I'M GRATEFUL FOR...

1

2

3

- ☐ MEDITATION
- ☐ YOGA
- ☐ EXERCISE
- ☐ ACKNOWLEDGEMENT
- ☐ AFFIRMATIONS
- ☐ _____

DREAMS FROM LAST NIGHT:

MY BEST 24-HOUR MOMENT:

TODAY, I WILL ACCOMPLISH...

TODAY, I WILL GROW BY...

For more inspiration, go to iamaluminary.com.

Manifestation Mantra:

DATE:

I'M GRATEFUL FOR...

1

2

3

- ☐ MEDITATION
- ☐ YOGA
- ☐ EXERCISE
- ☐ ACKNOWLEDGEMENT
- ☐ AFFIRMATIONS
- ☐ _____

DREAMS FROM LAST NIGHT:

MY BEST 24-HOUR MOMENT:

TODAY, I WILL ACCOMPLISH...

TODAY, I WILL GROW BY...

DATE:

I'M GRATEFUL FOR...

1

2

3

- ☐ MEDITATION
- ☐ YOGA
- ☐ EXERCISE
- ☐ ACKNOWLEDGEMENT
- ☐ AFFIRMATIONS
- ☐ _____

DREAMS FROM LAST NIGHT:

MY BEST 24-HOUR MOMENT:

TODAY, I WILL ACCOMPLISH...

TODAY, I WILL GROW BY...

For more inspiration, go to iamaluminary.com.

Manifestation Mantra:

DATE:

I'M GRATEFUL FOR...

1

2

3

- ☐ MEDITATION
- ☐ YOGA
- ☐ EXERCISE
- ☐ ACKNOWLEDGEMENT
- ☐ AFFIRMATIONS
- ☐ _____

DREAMS FROM LAST NIGHT:

MY BEST 24-HOUR MOMENT:

TODAY, I WILL ACCOMPLISH...

TODAY, I WILL GROW BY...

DATE:

I'M GRATEFUL FOR...

1

2

3

- ☐ MEDITATION
- ☐ YOGA
- ☐ EXERCISE
- ☐ ACKNOWLEDGEMENT
- ☐ AFFIRMATIONS
- ☐ _____

DREAMS FROM LAST NIGHT:

MY BEST 24-HOUR MOMENT:

TODAY, I WILL ACCOMPLISH...

TODAY, I WILL GROW BY...

For more inspiration, go to iamaluminary.com.

Manifestation Mantra:

DATE:

I'M GRATEFUL FOR…

1

2

3

- ☐ MEDITATION
- ☐ YOGA
- ☐ EXERCISE
- ☐ ACKNOWLEDGEMENT
- ☐ AFFIRMATIONS
- ☐ _____

DREAMS FROM LAST NIGHT:

MY BEST 24-HOUR MOMENT:

TODAY, I WILL ACCOMPLISH…

TODAY, I WILL GROW BY…

DATE:

I'M GRATEFUL FOR…

1

2

3

- ☐ MEDITATION
- ☐ YOGA
- ☐ EXERCISE
- ☐ ACKNOWLEDGEMENT
- ☐ AFFIRMATIONS
- ☐ _____

DREAMS FROM LAST NIGHT:

MY BEST 24-HOUR MOMENT:

TODAY, I WILL ACCOMPLISH…

TODAY, I WILL GROW BY…

Manifestation Mantra:

DATE:

I'M GRATEFUL FOR...

1

2

3

- ☐ MEDITATION
- ☐ YOGA
- ☐ EXERCISE
- ☐ ACKNOWLEDGEMENT
- ☐ AFFIRMATIONS
- ☐ _____

DREAMS FROM LAST NIGHT:

MY BEST 24-HOUR MOMENT:

TODAY, I WILL ACCOMPLISH...

TODAY, I WILL GROW BY...

DATE:

I'M GRATEFUL FOR...

1

2

3

- ☐ MEDITATION
- ☐ YOGA
- ☐ EXERCISE
- ☐ ACKNOWLEDGEMENT
- ☐ AFFIRMATIONS
- ☐ _____

DREAMS FROM LAST NIGHT:

MY BEST 24-HOUR MOMENT:

TODAY, I WILL ACCOMPLISH...

TODAY, I WILL GROW BY...